THE
WHEELS
OF JUSTICE

*The True Story Of A 27-Year Battle
To Convict My Sister's Killer*

RENEE FEHR
with Brian Whitney

WILDBLUE
PRESS

WildBluePress.com

THE WHEELS OF JUSTICE published by:
WILDBLUE PRESS
P.O. Box 102440
Denver, Colorado 80250

WILDBLUE PRESS is registered at the U.S. Patent and Trademark Offices.

ISBN 978-1-952225-76-5 Trade Paperback
ISBN 978-1-952225-75-8 eBook

Interior Formatting/Cover Design by Elijah Toten
www.totencreative.com

THE WHEELS OF JUSTICE

*"The wheels of justice turn slowly,
but grind exceedingly fine."*

This book is dedicated to all victims of domestic violence. Not only ones like Sheryl, her children, their children, and those of generations to come, but the not-so-obvious ones like the rest of the victim's family, including extended family, and friends. Until our society acknowledges domestic violence in its various forms and degrees and educates our children of their right to live free from it, domestic violence will not end and the often unrecognized, crippling ripple effects will continue.

INTRODUCTION

There was no mystery as to who murdered my sister, Sheryl. I knew Greg Houser was going to kill her.

On October 25,1990, he entered the home they used to share and strangled her to death. Then, he dragged her body across the floor and out to the garage. Next, he wrapped a rope around her neck and hung her from a pipe between the rafters, one that he used to dress deer. He had once threatened her that if she crossed him, that if she didn't do what he said, he would do this very thing to her. He placed a ladder next to her body, to make it look like suicide.

I told numerous people this would happen. I told Sheryl's divorce lawyer Greg was going to kill her. Just a few days before she was murdered, I told my secretary I was afraid he was going to kill her. And of course, my mother, my other two sisters, and I all talked daily about the possibility of her being murdered during our numerous, panicked phone calls.

I never liked Greg. No one in my family did. It wasn't just because of the type of person he was, which was certainly bad enough. It was that he didn't respect my sister. He was cruel to her, and because of that, at least in part, she was sad. While Sheryl appeared happy enough on the surface, inside of her I suspected there was great pain. I saw it in her eyes. I heard it in her voice. Yet, she never talked about her feelings around her marriage and I never asked.

I was positive of one thing though, even without her telling me. Greg was awful to her. I often saw him pick on her until she cried. I knew he was capable of great cruelty, but I couldn't fathom the true darkness that came to be their marriage.

It took my mother being diagnosed with cancer in June of 1990 for Sheryl to take action. She confided in me, as well as my sisters, that she wanted to leave Greg and she had for a long time, but she knew she needed our mother by her side to give her strength. Short of the boys being abused, she might never have left Greg; but when my mother was diagnosed, Sheryl knew the time was now. She needed our mother's help and support to make this move.

I always had my doubts about her relationship with Greg, right from the very start. Sheryl was the oldest in the family and the first to date. Greg was not kind to her even then, but as young and naïve as I was, I thought the way Greg acted toward her perhaps was the way all young men treated young women.

He wasn't a warm person, or kind. Rather, he was the macho type who liked big trucks, loud engines, and fast cars. He wasn't nice to Sheryl, not even in front of us. He often made fun of her, not in a fun-loving sort of way, but in a way that brought tears to her eyes and sometimes made her cry.

But we weren't the ones dating him, so in our mind, our place was to respect our sister and her choices. So, we didn't say anything. People didn't talk about such things in the late 80s/early 90s in small town Illinois, especially in a family such as mine. We just kept our mouths shut and hoped for the best. Yet, the signs of what was to come were there, we just missed them or chose to ignore them; I'm really not sure. Sometimes the signs were glaring.

Cats on our farm were a dime a dozen. I can remember times when we could count over 30 cats that lived with us. But every now and then a special one came along who captured our hearts and became more than a number and became a family member. Boots was one of those cats.

One day he went missing. I thought he would come back soon but as the hours turned into days, I knew he was probably never coming back. I was heartbroken.

I looked for him for days, walking around the barn lot calling "Here kitty, kitty!" but to no avail. My whole family joined in looking for him. Greg and a friend of his who was dating my sister, Lisa, even helped us with the search one day.

Finally, Greg's friend took pity on me and told me to give up on the search. The cat wasn't coming back. It was dead. Greg shot Boots and tossed him in the pasture for the coyotes to devour. All because he committed the crime of walking across his freshly washed car which pissed him off.

This despicable act turned my feelings towards Greg from dislike to hatred. But still, Sheryl was my sister and if he made her happy, I wasn't going to say anything. I didn't know what to do. I decided if my sister liked him, it was her business and not mine and I would keep quiet and not cause trouble. It had taken her a long time to find a boyfriend and she seemed generally happy. I didn't want to ruin that for her.

But years later, once Sheryl made up her mind about leaving Greg, it didn't take long for her to act. One day in July, Sheryl called and asked me if I knew any good divorce attorneys. I suggested a lawyer I knew to be good. It was more than apparent Sheryl was going to need someone to fight for her. Greg was not going to go quietly.

To no one's surprise, Greg didn't take the news well. He was furious and told her if she left him, he would make sure he got custody of the kids. He and Sheryl had three young boys. Every time he made this type of threat, it stopped her in her tracks. Her children meant everything to her.

Greg was sexually abusive to Sheryl. He treated her like his slave in the bedroom. Even in the early days, before I knew the true nightmare of their marriage, she said that if she didn't have sex with Greg every day, he became furious.

She could handle that, she could even deal with how awful he was to her, but what she couldn't cope with was how he treated the kids, and how worse she feared things might become later for them with continued exposure to Greg.

During the process of Sheryl leaving Greg, I felt enormous stress. Every day, Sheryl called and reported to me events and her accomplishments. She slowly started to reveal to me all the horrible things he was doing to her. I gasped silently when I heard the abuse described but tried to remain calm and unemotional so I could be the best help and support to her possible. I made recommendations of things she should do as if she was a client, and not my sister, and she would dutifully complete them. The tasks were many and varied. Go to counseling. Keep a journal. Write everything down. Prepare to be on your own. Get your own credit card. Make plans to lower your expenses. Go get drug tested.

It never failed. After I was done listening to Sheryl and advising her that day, my mother called and I'd have to listen to it all over again from my mother's perspective. "Do you know what Greg has accused Sheryl of now? Do you know what Greg said? Do you know what Greg did? Have you talked to Sheryl? Did she tell you these things? What did you tell her? What are you going to do? How can you fix this? How can you make this better?"

I didn't have the heart to tell my mother that I'd heard it all, directly from Sheryl. It was obvious to me that Mom wanted to vent and needed my support and assurance that everything was going to be okay as much as, if not more than, Sheryl did. I tried to act as if they were just clients so I could provide the most objective, independent, and helpful advice I knew how. What I didn't realize at the time was that trying to maintain this persona was very taxing on me both physically and emotionally.

It wasn't just that I was always the person in the family who tried to make things right for everyone that caused them to lean on me. I also was a lawyer, which to my family meant I had the ability and the knowledge to figure out how to solve every problem that came up. Whether or not they ever expressed that expectation to me, it is the expectation I told myself they had of me. The pressure I placed on myself was enormous.

I was only 25 years old and was beginning my second year practicing law 1,800 miles away from home. I did my best to juggle work while at the same time attempting to deflate everyone's stress, which, of course, just made my own stress level rise even more.

It all was too much. I had to fix this for Sheryl. I had to fix it for my mom. And I had to fix it for myself to preserve the image I had painted of my perfect family in my head.

I got permission to talk directly to her attorney. Perhaps I could make things better and do so faster if I could speak directly to him. He was a lawyer with a lot of experience who was used to doing things his own way. I am sure he was offended by me calling and questioning him and demanding to know what action he was going to take, but he never said a word about my calls, questions, or suggestions. In hindsight, I'm not sure I could have done that if the tables were turned and I was the experienced attorney being questioned by a young attorney who was a family member of his client.

After she told Greg she wanted out, he filed for divorce. Even though she was the one that wanted to be gone, there was no way he would give her the satisfaction of filing before him. Despite his outward claim that he wanted a divorce, in private he begged her to stop breaking up their marriage and their family. He begged her to come back to him.

Each day, Greg became angrier and more threatening and erratic. She got an order of protection, but it was worthless. Greg was nothing but irrational, and he had no interest in playing by the rules. In those days, even if there were abuse allegations, it wasn't talked about, especially in small town Illinois. Whatever happened in your house happened in your house, and there wasn't much attention paid to it by those on the outside. It was the unspoken rule that these things were not to be discussed outside the home by anyone.

The calls from Sheryl continued, sometimes multiple times a day. But now, things were changing. She was more open with the details and she was moving on from, "I can handle him" to "I'm afraid of him". In the beginning, the fear she expressed was about him taking her babies away from her. As time went on, the fear she expressed was about what he would do to her. That fear eventually turned to terror, which worried me because Sheryl was never a dramatic person. I was the dramatic person who was trying hard to hold it all together for her, but when I heard the fear in her voice, I internalized a feeling that was foreign to me.

I knew deep down something bad was going to happen to her. I was doing everything I could to keep it from occurring, yet I knew I really didn't have control over the outcome. I knew before it happened that I was going to be a failure in her eyes and my family's eyes but I didn't know what to do other than try harder, work harder, and put in longer hours on her case. I had no one to talk to. While I was married, my husband wasn't emotionally supportive of me during this time. He never asked me what was going on and I never told him because I knew that's not what he wanted to talk about.

Despite the fact Greg wasn't telling the truth about anything, he always seemed to have the upper hand. We were in a battle with someone who had absolutely no morals, and no qualms about saying, or doing, anything to win. Which is one of the many things that made him so dangerous.

Some of the abuse towards Sheryl involved his friends, a couple of degenerate townies named Les and T-Byrd. He often did his dirty work with one of them around so they could be a witness for him. One night, he and my sister got in a fight in the basement. Greg threw her to the floor, sat on her chest, and started to sexually assault her. She began screaming for someone to help her.

While Greg was molesting her. Les was upstairs hanging out, listening to it all go on. He was there to be Greg's witness so Greg could say nothing happened and that Sheryl was crazy if she decided to tell anyone.

It was insane.

One question kept coming back to me in my mind. How would this end? Greg had threatened Sheryl that if she didn't come back to him, he would fight her to the end, and he would win.

Greg wouldn't allow himself to lose, and I didn't know what winning looked like to him anymore. He didn't want there to be a divorce because that was loss of control and it would make him look bad. But there was no way Sheryl could stay with him. The abuse was too much. She could never raise her children in that horrific environment with that monster. Eventually, she knew he would abuse her babies, which was truly her worst fear.

By this time, we had seen Greg yell at the boys and call them sissies when they cried. We saw how terrified of him they were. We knew he had spanked the oldest boy so hard for getting out of bed one night that he peed the bed.

I didn't know what I could do for her. The main thing was to support her in making sure he couldn't have the children because, God forbid, if he got custody of them, he would abuse them too.

Three weeks before she died, it finally happened. Greg tried to kill her.

It was Greg's turn to take care of the kids. Their youngest had asthma, Greg called Sheryl and said their son seemed to be having some difficulty breathing. Being the concerned mother that she was, she came to the house.

He tricked her into going into the bedroom. When she saw ropes attached to the headboard, she knew she was in trouble. She tried to run out of the room, but he grabbed her and forced her onto the bed. He tied her hands to the headboard and gagged her by stuffing the bed sheets in her mouth. Then Greg, the man she married and bore children with, sat on her chest and began to sexually assault her. He held the rope across her mouth, leaving rope burns on her cheeks as she fought and struggled.

After he did what he wanted to, my sister managed to talk him down a bit to the point that she was able to free her hands from the ropes. He told her he wouldn't let her go until she wrote on a piece of paper he handed to her that she consented to have sex with him.

Once free, she ran a quarter mile to a neighbor's house and banged on the door in hysterics. They called the police who promptly arrested Greg. He was charged with Aggravated Attempted Sexual Assault and quickly bailed out. Sheryl was questioned by the police then treated in the emergency room where they took pictures of her injuries.

She later told me when she was tied to that bed, gagged and helpless, she looked into his eyes and knew for the first time that Greg could kill her. That it might happen.

As incredibly awful as this was, there was a bit of a silver lining when it came to the divorce and custody battle. I told Sheryl that sometimes something unimaginably bad has to happen before things can change.

Yes, this was horrific, but she survived. There was no way he was going to get the kids now. She was going to win. I really thought that I had won too and would be successful in my family's eyes.

Everything quickly fell into place. An emergency order was issued stating Greg couldn't live in the house any longer. Sheryl was granted temporary custody of the children, the house, and financial support. It was over.

Sheryl was becoming more confident. Almost cocky really. She wasn't as afraid of him anymore. In her mind, he wasn't going to get away with all of the horrible things he did. He had been arrested and was proven a liar. Things were going to get better. I had told her that the custody case was over—she had obtained custody and that wasn't going to change. He still kept harassing her and begging her to return but things seemed to have stopped escalating.

Somehow, after all of this, Greg still believed he could change her mind and continued to beg her to take him back. My family and I thought this was bizarre, why would he think Sheryl would possibly get back with him after all he had done?

As bad as things became, it seemed like the worst was over. Greg had outed himself as the monster he truly was. Sheryl was going to get custody of her children and she was going to get divorced. Her dirty laundry had been aired for all to see so she had no more shame around any of it. She had a network of family and friends who were supporting her. Soon Greg would be gone, and our fairy tale life would continue because Sheryl was certainly justified in my eyes and the eyes of our family and church. No one could be expected to live with him under the circumstances that had now been exposed and with the upcoming trial would be publicly outed.

But there was one thing I couldn't get out of my mind. When it comes to someone like this, what does "over" really mean? How could someone like this stop? He told her he would win, and he certainly hadn't won so how could it really be over?

The state's case against Greg for the aggravated criminal sexual assault was proceeding. He pressured her to drop the charges and not to testify against him. He told her if she did, he would "string her fucking up" from a tree in the front yard like he did the deer he killed and dressed. What he didn't understand is that it wasn't her decision to make as to whether the case proceeded against him. The State's Attorney made that decision. Of course, if a victim didn't want to cooperate with the State's Attorney or wasn't available to testify, the State may not pursue the charges.

It felt like the calm before the storm. On the outside, I exuded confidence in Shery's situation. On the inside, I was still terrified he was going to kill her. It ran through my mind all day and invaded my dreams at night. He would kill her for revenge and to stay out of prison. If she wasn't there to testify, there was no case against him, he would get custody of the kids, and he wouldn't have to pay child support.

He would murder her. How else would this end? He would not be defeated and with her alive he could not win.

The night before my sister died, she called and told me she was going to take her maiden name back. She was happy about how angry that would make him. I was glad she was taking back her name, and the power that came with it, but Greg was so crazy it didn't make sense to me for her to tell him. Especially if she thought it would make him angry. But I didn't say anything to her. She had been through such torment she deserved some happiness and her own little celebration.

On the morning of October 5, 1990, I was sitting in my office behind my big wooden desk engulfed in burgundy leather, working for the law firm of Cobb Cole & Bell in Daytona Beach, Florida. I had just reached a settlement on a case; one that had been dragging on for months. It was a big success for me, and I was proud of my work.

As I worked, I felt the presence of someone in the room. I looked up to see my husband, John, standing in the doorway wearing shorts and a tee shirt. I was confused for a moment. I was at work. He didn't belong in my doorway.

Then I knew. I screamed, "He killed her, didn't he!"

I jumped up with such force that my awkward and heavy chair spun away like a child's toy and crashed into a credenza behind me. I ran into John's arms screaming, "I told you he was going to kill her, I told everyone he was going to kill her!" John could only nod his head and hold me tight.

Earlier that day, one of my sisters called John and told him "Sheryl is dead. One of the boys found her hanging in the garage."

That morning at the hospital where Sheryl worked, a co-worker who knew just enough about her personal situation was worried when she didn't show up for her 7:00 a.m. shift. She called Sheryl's house to check on her. The first time, no one answered. She waited a few minutes and called back and Sheryl's oldest son answered the phone. When the nurse asked him if she could speak to his mommy, he said, "I don't know where my mommy is."

She then said, "Put down the phone, go find your mommy, and tell her that someone at work needs to speak with her. If you can't find your mommy, come back and tell me that."

After what seemed like an eternity, Sheryl's oldest came back to the phone and announced, "I found Mommy. She is asleep in the garage with a rope around her neck and I can't wake her up."

The co-worker dialed 911.

Sheryl's body was found on the garage floor with her upper torso held up by thin yellow nylon boating rope which had been looped over a piece of metal pipe placed across the rafters and used by Greg to hang and dress deer that he hunted and killed. A tall stepladder was found in an upright position near her body. The rope was tied three times around her neck.

She had not given anyone any indication she was despondent or depressed. There was no suicide note. When I last spoke to her she seemed happier than she had been in months.

It made sense she left no note. The thought of Sheryl killing herself never crossed my mind.

ONE

When I was a child, my life felt like a fairy tale.

My family lived a simple life; one without any extravagances, but we wanted for nothing. We lived in an old white farmhouse in the country outside of Farmer City, Illinois, a small town with a population of around 2,000. My dad was the tenant farmer on a 900-acre farm.

I was the third of four daughters. My father was a hard-working man of few words, my mother was a nurse. She was a strong woman who liked helping others and lived for her children.

My mom and dad are both from small towns in Illinois. My dad grew up on a farm outside of Eureka, Illinois milking cows. He was a very quiet and stoic man when I was growing up. My father had a great sense of humor, but he didn't show it to just anyone.

He worked the farm we lived on all by himself, raising cows and pigs, and growing corn and soybeans. He was out the door before 6 in the morning and worked until well after the sun went down. My mother rang a bell when it was dinnertime to let him know it was time to come in. He replied with a whistle to indicate he would be in shortly.

Sheryl and I often spent time on the farm with our dad. We loved to ride on the tractor or the combine with him and often stayed on it until it was time to come in for supper. We spent most of our time playing outdoors, even if the weather wasn't all that nice. Even though it smelled, it was always warm in the pig barn where baby pigs were being born and there were always chores that needed to be done. The rabbits needed their cage cleaned and to be fed and to have fresh water. The cats and dogs needed food and water along with the feeding of other random pets such as ducks and chickens. My mom worked nights at the local nursing home so she could stay home with us during the day. Back then I had no idea the sacrifices my parents were making for us. On some days before my older sisters got home from school, she had me and my little sister sit on top of her while we watched TV on the couch while she took a nap so she could catch up on her sleep. It was an ingenious method; if we got off of her, she would wake up and tell us to get back up on the couch.

We only got three TV channels on a good day, we still had a party line phone, and computers and video games were nonexistent. That meant nothing to us because we spent all our time outside with our myriad of farm animals and pets.

Sheryl never met an animal that she couldn't nurse back from near death or tame. Tiny Tim, the racoon, loved being fed with a baby bottle. In exchange, he tolerated being dressed in doll clothes and pushed around in a baby buggy. Petunia the goat raced around the yard with us, chased cars along with the dogs, and snuggled with us at night. Alfie, the pet cow, laid at the back door with the dogs, greeted us when we got off the bus and made a great pillow to lean up against on the Saturdays my mom worked.

There was very little conflict or drama at our home. Our parents' expectations were clear. Work hard, get an education, and a good life would follow. So, we did. My oldest sister, Sheryl, wanted to be a nurse like my mom. It was no surprise that she wanted to substitute humans for all the animals she nursed and cared for while growing up. Lisa was the planner and organizer and second homemaker to my mom. As an adult, she started her career in the hospitality industry. Julie's plan was to follow in both Mom's and

Sheryl's footsteps and be a nurse but seek an advanced nursing degree.

I was born a peacekeeper and problem solver. My freshman year of high school I announced to my family I was going to be a lawyer. No one who knew me was really shocked, but still, it was a lofty goal for a girl from Farmer City. But it never crossed my mind that I might not achieve it. Once I decided I was going to do something, I did it and that was that.

We were driven to succeed but we had no idea what we were doing was hard work. We didn't know any different. My sisters and I have often wondered where we got our drive because growing up it never seemed like we were pushed by our parents. Perhaps we were and just never realized it.

I don't remember knowing any boys until I went to a wiener roast at the neighbors at which John, my future husband, was at with his parents. We lived in the country and spent most of our time playing with each other and when we did play with others, all of our country neighbors and family friends had little girls. We didn't really think about boys until Sheryl turned sixteen.

Sheryl was a senior in high school when someone finally took interest in her. Greg grew up in Mansfield, Illinois, which was a town of around 800 occupants. The towns were both too small to support schools from kindergarten through high school independently so the kids from both towns went to the same junior high school in Mansfield and the same high school in Farmer City. There was no real story that I recall of how they met, our classes were small, and they interacted and had mutual friends from seventh grade on. There were only 60 or so students in her class so there wasn't a large number of boys to choose from.

We were excited for our big sister to have a boyfriend that came to the house, taking some of the spotlight off of me and Lisa who weren't quite as obedient as Sheryl, the first born. It was also exciting to have an older boy around who occasionally came by with other male friends close to our ages.

Greg was a simple person. He liked girls, fast cars, and big trucks. Like a lot of high school boys from our area, Greg oozed macho.

His dad owned a gas station in Mansfield and was the local auto mechanic. Greg's ambition was to go to the local junior college and become a diesel mechanic which is what he, in fact, ended up doing with his life. His idea of a good time was to take his big truck with its oversized wheels and go 4-wheeling, slinging mud everywhere. The muddier his truck was when he was rolling back into town, the more you knew what a good time he had raising hell.

He often came to the house in his gold Trans Am to pick Sheryl up for their dates. When I turned 16, he even let me take his car into town to pick something up at the store. I cruised around Main Street and then went to the library parking lot so I could do something I had always wanted to do—squeal the tires and burn rubber on the road like I had seen him do so many times. The car had way more power than I imagined and while I knew it looked like fun when other people left burn outs, I had no idea how exciting the adrenaline rush would be. My heart was racing and my palms were sweating, but I had a smile so big I didn't know if it ever would go away. I worried when I got home that he would know what I had done just by the look on my face.

He had won my sister over. Sheryl was smitten with Greg, to say the least. On that day in the library parking lot, with black smoke rolling behind me, he won me over for a bit too. Greg frequently reminded me of the day he let me drive his car and how he was going to let me do it again someday, but he never did.

It wasn't long before cracks in his armor started to show. He liked the attention he got from all of us girls and began to act cocky in front of us. Before long, he spent a lot of time teasing Sheryl in our presence and making fun of her.

He did a lot of things to Sheryl that I know now are signs of abuse. He often put down her body and her looks, not only in private, but in front of other people. He tickled her, even after she asked him to stop. No matter how long she took getting ready or what new outfit she put on for him he always found a flaw in her and pointed it out to her in front of us and anyone else that may have been around.

I came to expect Greg's criticism of Sheryl, followed by seeing the fading of my sister's smile. I could see the hurt in her eyes grow stronger and deeper with every public berating she received about something he saw wrong with her that no one else ever seemed to notice.

I didn't like it, but I didn't have much perspective when it came to Sheryl or boys in general for that matter. Greg's behavior was noticeable enough that Lisa and I would occasionally make comments to each other about the fact he just didn't seem very nice to Sheryl and no matter what she did it was never good enough for him. But we were young and more than a little bit sheltered. We had no point of reference to know that all boys didn't treat girls they were dating that way. Besides that, she was our older sister and if she liked him, we assumed there must have been a redeeming quality about him that we just didn't get to see.

There were many more signs of serious character flaws with Greg, but I was young and self-absorbed. I eventually accepted the fact that I was never going to get to drive that shiny gold Trans Am again and didn't pay much attention to him anymore. Greg's novelty wore off along with the finish on his car as the years went by.

After high school, it didn't take long before Sheryl became engaged to Greg, who was the one and only real boyfriend she ever had. It was no surprise to any of us. She was going to be a nurse, get married, and have babies. Greg was her boyfriend and that was it. Sheryl finished nurse's training, living in the basement of our Aunt Kathy's house.

But there continued to be signs of unhappiness. Often there were tears shed by Sheryl, followed by Greg storming out the door, and still later flowers being delivered to the door with a follow up letter in the mail which all contained the same message. Greg wouldn't have "gotten mad" if Sheryl wouldn't have done "X". You fill in the blank.

She graduated in May and they were married in June in the Catholic church in Farmer City. My sister, Lisa, and I were both in the wedding party.

The reception was at a place called the Moose Lodge. The day after the wedding, the owners of the lodge had to call my dad because the night of the reception their iconic stuffed moose head disappeared from the wall. Greg and Sheryl had left town that night and stayed in a hotel for a couple nights for their honeymoon. Lisa and I found the moose head on a shelf in their home and returned it to the lodge.

Sheryl had never lived on her own until marriage. She and Greg rented a little tenant house on a farm next door to the big farmhouse where the owners lived. Their son, Brandon, was born nine months after the honeymoon. I vividly remember how happy she was being pregnant and the smile on her face when she brought her first little boy home. She had always dreamed of being a mother. I was in college when her first was born but I still got to see him fairly regularly.

Sheryl struggled in nursing school. It wasn't easy for her. But she graduated and became a nurse in the neonatal unit of a local hospital. She loved her work. She could nurse all of those struggling newborns back to health just like she did with the baby animals she rescued growing up.

Her second boy was born three years later. I was away at law school when she brought her second beloved boy home with a smile on her face that radiated from deep within her. I was a little jealous of my sister, Lisa, because she lived close by and got to spend time with Sheryl and her boys and play "Aunt", which looked like so much fun. When I came home for holidays and visits, I couldn't wait to go to Sheryl's house and play with the boys. In my mind, it was all a continuation of my fairy tale life. I would drop in on my married sister, play with my cute nephews in their cute little house, take pictures to memorialize the moment, and go back to law school.

I didn't realize that what I thought was a fairy tale was more like the beginnings of a horror story. The signs were there, I just didn't have the perspective to read and understand them.

All of a sudden, Sheryl didn't like me to come to her house. I could tell that it was torture for her when I stopped by unannounced.

If Greg was there, it was obvious how annoyed he was that I was intruding. He made it so uncomfortable for me, my sisters, and the boys that I would quickly find an excuse to leave. If he wasn't there, she couldn't be happier that I had dropped in to see her and her precious boys but while I was there it was clear how nervous she was, wondering when he would get home and whether my presence was going to make him angry.

Sheryl was proud of her home and accepted any help we offered in decorating, cleaning, and just making the house a home. One day, I offered to help her hang pictures on the dining room wall. She appreciated my help, but she was worried what Greg might say if he came home while we were hammering nails into the wall. As we worked, she kept looking out the window at the driveway. When she finally saw his truck pull in, she grabbed the hammer out of my hand, set the picture I was about to hang on the floor, and told me to go. I could feel her terror emanating off of her.

After her third son was born just two years later, I was home from Florida and was invited over to meet and hold her newest bundle of joy. The other two boys were lively and glad to see their Aunt Renee. I sat in her home holding the baby and watching the other two play. Greg was outside mowing the lawn, so Sheryl was more at ease with me being around than usual.

Suddenly, the front door burst open, I looked up and saw Greg was out of breath and flushed with excitement. I couldn't imagine what could possible cause such a physical reaction while mowing the lawn. He yelled at the oldest, "Come on, I found a bunny's nest in the yard!"

For a split second I thought, "how sweet, he wants to show his son the baby bunnies". Then in that same second, he shattered that thought by finishing his sentence with, "I want you to ride with me when I mow over it." I had flashbacks of Boots and wondered if he had gotten that excited when he killed him. I felt I might throw up as I thought about him being so excited about mutilating baby bunnies with the lawn mower that he wanted his five-year-old to experience it with him. Sheryl and I exchanged a quick glance. The look she gave me said, "I'm sorry, but there is nothing I can do." I didn't say a word because I didn't want to make her life any worse than it already appeared to be. My hatred of him deepened, but I continued to tell myself I wasn't married to him and it wasn't any of my business.

Soon our family stopped dropping by Sheryl's house. It caused us all more stress than it was worth. She still wanted to see us and share her precious boys with her family, so we all waited for her to visit us at our homes instead. Greg stopped coming to family events, but she always had an excuse for the reasons why. Before too long she started missing some family events herself.

Other odd things began to happen. Sheryl was always a bit uncoordinated, but it seemed since her marriage to Greg she became more so. She ran into a door and bruised her jaw. She opened a cabinet and hit her face which caused her to have a black eye. Her best friend, Julie, later told me that she chose a high-neck wedding dress despite it being summer to hide bruises she anticipated having on her neck.

She didn't do much anymore but go to work, take care of her boys, and visit us occasionally. We all noticed the changes but again we didn't say a word. Far be it for any of us to cause problems in our sister's marriage.

When we did see them together, we all walked on eggshells and tiptoed around him. We wanted him to be happy because it was so uncomfortable for everyone if he wasn't, but we wanted her to be happy too. It was impossible to know what mood he was going to be in and what to do. On the rare occasions we all got together, Greg was always looking at his watch until he would finally snap out to Sheryl, "Let's go. Get the kids. Let's go!" When this happened, we would all scurry around to get her and the kids ready, out the door, and into the car before he totally lost it and started screaming at her.

Sheryl was so proud of me when I graduated from law school. She and her oldest son made the trip to Florida along with my parents to watch me graduate. The sun glistened in the courtyard of Stetson University that day, which added the perfect touch to my fairy tale life. Shortly after holding my diploma high above my head and taking pictures, my parents, Sheryl and her oldest, and I headed across the state to Daytona. We dropped my things from my small dorm room at the law school in John's apartment in Daytona Beach. As I had dreamed, I married after law school and began my own family. John caught my eye at the wiener roast years before. He was my first date and we continued to date off and on until my junior year of high school. He asked me to go to his senior prom with him. I was excited, accepted, picked out the perfect dress and had it hemmed. I was so excited waiting for the prom to come when he called a few days before the big day and told me he really wanted to go with Kris, my sister's friend, but he had asked his friend Paul to take me. I was heartbroken but I went to prom with Paul.

As if graduation and Christmas wouldn't have made the month stressful enough, my wedding was planned for

December 30th in Bloomington, so after a brief stop in Daytona at John's apartment, we started the journey back to Illinois. So far, my life had been planned perfectly and pretty much played out without a hitch. I had graduated from law school, now I would get married, have my own babies, and live happily ever after.

John and I reunited after a gun John was holding discharged accidently and killed Kris. I vividly remember standing in the kitchen when Lisa got the call from another one of their friends about the incident. Lisa was crying when she got off the phone and told me what had happened.

I felt a knot in my stomach and told Lisa, "John is going to call me and I don't know what to say to him."

Sure enough, he called. As soon as he told me what happened, I started comforting him and vowed to help him recover from this tragic accident and get his life back on track. This was during my junior year of college. I had already made plans to attend law school at Washington University in St. Louis. As I was getting ready to start my senior year in college, John, with my strong encouragement, had decided that farming with his father wasn't going to get him what he wanted in life and he decided to attend Park's Aviation College of St. Louis University and obtain his Airframe and Powerplant certificate to be an aircraft mechanic. It was at Parks that he realized that his dream to become a professional pilot could really happen.

As I was finishing my first year of law school and John was completing his second year at Parks, he decided to transfer to sunny Florida and complete a four-year education at Embry Riddle Aeronautical University in aviation business management with the dream of becoming a professional pilot one day.

This would become a pattern for us. John would decide what he wanted to do, announce it to me, and I would follow along supporting him. So, when he decided he wanted to finish school in Daytona and the thought of being without him was not an option for me, I did the impossible and transferred to Stetson University College of Law in St. Petersburg, Florida.

We had never discussed living away from our families and I never had any intent of doing so, but if John wanted to do something, I followed dutifully along if I wanted to be with him.

Christmas came and went along with our wedding. John and I settled in his student apartment in Daytona Beach. I got a job as law clerk in a well-established Florida law firm since I hadn't taken the bar exam and John had another semester at ERAU. I always thought that soon after John got his degree we would move back home. In the meantime, I took the bar exam and passed it, then was offered an associate attorney position with the firm where I had been a clerk at a good salary. Pilot positions were hard to come by because of the high number of flight hours being required to gain employment and the expense of building those hours. We were fortunate because John was also an aircraft mechanic. Upon his graduation, he was offered a job as a mechanic and a co-pilot of a lifeline helicopter off the top of the hospital in Melbourne, Florida. He wasn't going to be paid much, but I had a good job and could afford for him to take this job with hopes of building the hours he needed.

We moved to a condominium on the Intercoastal in Titusville, Florida where we looked across the water at the Kennedy Space Center. We had front row seats to the space shuttle launches from a screened-in balcony. John drove an hour south to his job and I drove an hour north to mine. Not long after we moved to Titusville, the owner of the company John was working for offered him an opportunity in his Fort Lauderdale operation as a mechanic with the enticement of building hours in a Lear jet. Fort Lauderdale was too far to commute daily so John lived there during the week and we took turns going back and forth on the weekends.

Meanwhile, I still drove daily back and forth to Daytona to my job.

I missed my family dearly. I hated missing out on what the rest of the family was doing.

Sheryl had three small boys, a job, and a difficult husband that I knew she spent a great deal of time trying to please. I think she was happy. At least that was my impression from the pictures she sent me.

We didn't talk much anymore.

TWO

In 1990, at the end of May, my mom visited me in Florida. While this was not her first time visiting, it was the first time since I graduated from law school and had gotten married. She wanted to see our new home and where I was working. This trip was special. Lisa had just had her first child, Allison, in October of 1989, a couple months after Sheryl had given birth to her third little boy. Julie, the youngest of my sisters, was recently married, so for the first time, my mother and father were alone in an empty house. My mother was in her early 50s and was ready to live for herself for once. One of the first things she did to enjoy her newfound freedom was to spend time with me at my condo overlooking the Intercoastal.

It was special to have her with me all to myself in my new home in my new town. I was excited and proud to take her into the office to see where I worked and to meet my boss and coworkers. I took her to my favorite restaurants, we spent time shopping and exploring Titusville and lounged by my building's pool on the intercoastal waterway, watching the dolphins play and the manatees swim by. When we sat on my balcony soaking in the serene view of the river with the shuttle launch pads in the background, I couldn't help but dream about more moments like this and the day my mom would visit me and our children we planned to have in a few years.

I still cherish that visit because they were the first and final memories of having a mom like I thought I would have in my adult life—a mom who spent time with me, who was interested in my life and what I was doing. These were the last days I spent with my mom before all of this happened, before Sheryl was murdered. They were the first and last days I spent with her when I could enjoy her company as my mother and my friend. They were the last days her grandchildren were still innocent to the horrible things that happen in this world. My mother was never the same afterwards.

Once she returned home, she began spending more time with Sheryl and her children. One day, she complained to Sheryl that her neck was stiff and had been for some time. Always the caregiver, Sheryl began rubbing Mom's neck, hoping to give her some relief from her discomfort. As she gave our mom a massage, she discovered a lump on her clavicle. Sheryl was instantly worried and convinced my mom to make a doctor's appointment right away.

The doctor found the lump concerning and set my mother up to undergo a battery of tests. My sisters, my father, and I were all extremely anxious. We feared cancer and none of us could bear the thought of seeing our mom, who had always been the caregiver, suffer from that dreaded disease, need care from others, and possibly die.

Our lives revolved around our mom. She was our comfort, reassurance, and support, and we were hers. Even though she rarely verbalized them, we always knew she had high expectations of us, and we wanted to live up to her expectations. We wanted her approval. We wanted her to be proud of us, and she was. We all needed her when we were children, and in some ways, we needed her even more as adults. We never dreamed how much she would eventually need all of us.

Eventually, she had a biopsy and was told it was cancer. This was devastating to all of us. When I heard the news,

I sunk to the floor and sobbed. During this time, I talked on the phone constantly to my sisters as we tried to support each other through our sorrow and fear. I couldn't even fathom what it would be like to live without my mom. Being without her had never crossed my mind.

I spoke to Sheryl most often in the days to come, not just because she was my sister but because she was a nurse and I highly respected her opinions on my mother's health. Sheryl was distraught by the news but no more so than the rest of us. Every day we talked on the phone discussing all the "what ifs."

It was good we had each other as an outlet for our sorrows, because Greg wasn't there emotionally to support her and John physically wasn't present to support me. Quite the opposite actually. There was no loving husband for Sheryl to lean on for comfort and support. When Sheryl cried in front of Greg, it angered him. So much so, that he would forcefully tell her to stop. Of course, that only made matters worse.

One night shortly after we received the devastating news, the phone rang, it was Greg on the line. I was surprised to hear from him. This was the first time he had ever called me in their seven years of marriage. For a moment, I thought he was calling to be supportive but that was quickly driven from my mind as soon as he began to speak. He proceeded to tell me that he was sick and tired of Sheryl crying all the time, it was driving him crazy. Apparently, my mother's diagnosis was a big inconvenience to him. Sheryl's attention was being diverted from him, he didn't like it one bit, and he wanted me to make it stop.

But that wasn't all, he continued on to say it was my mother's "own damn fault" she had cancer because she knew the lump was there for a long time and she didn't do anything about it. He finished this conversation by telling me the doctors had done some more tests on my mother and found two spots on her spine and things looked really bad for her.

Oddly, in this same conversation, Greg told me that "Your sister and I are almost ready to split up over this. I can't stand her crying." It struck me how strange and out of context that comment was. I responded by telling Greg that this news was hard on all of us and it was a time when all of us needed to pull together and help each other through.

If I had not just gotten off the phone with Sheryl, what Greg just told me on the phone would have sent me into a tailspin. However, Sheryl had just told me that yes, our mother had additional tests done at the Mayo Clinic, but the doctors were almost sure the spots were signs of degenerative disk disease caused by aging and arthritis and not cancer after all. When Sheryl called me and told me the news it was like our prayers were answered.

Why would Greg lie to me to try to make me feel more worry and pain? Did he call just to hurt me? Was he really that bad of a person? It seemed that was the case.

While my mother was not going to die from cancer, Sheryl's marriage was on life support. This experience shone a light on how Greg was simply not a good husband or friend, and someone that she could not count on in times of stress. It made Sheryl realize she was going to need her mother's support when it came time for what she considered to be an inevitable divorce and she decided she had to act while she knew she was healthy.

While one family crisis was averted, another was soon to follow. In early July, my sister, Lisa, was visiting me in Florida when Sheryl called and asked if I knew a good divorce attorney. She was leaving Greg. Once again, I was stunned. After I got off the phone with Sheryl, Lisa and I sat on the floor and cried. Although I had never thought highly of Greg to say the least, I wanted dearly for Greg and Sheryl to work out her problems for the children's sake.

I told Sheryl she had to go to counseling and try to work it out. We were Catholic, which, to me, meant that divorce was not an option no matter how bad things became; you simply made your marriage work. I had no idea he was physically abusing her, I just thought he was a jerk. I was a fixer by nature and my role in the family had become the solver of all family problems. I decided I would again rise to the occasion and help Sheryl fix her marriage.

Even though I felt they should try to stay together because they married each other and they had children, it wasn't like Greg was much of a father. Greg didn't spend much time with his kids, to him it was a woman's job to take care of them, and to take care of him as well. His involvement as a father was slim to none. He didn't take them to any appointments, he wouldn't read to them or give them a bath, he pretty much never had them alone. He would come home from work, and expect dinner to be on the table, then he would sit around and watch TV and drink beer unless he went to Jim's Tap, the local bar, which he did at least three or four times a week.

Sheryl had already told Greg of her plans for divorce before I became aware of the situation. Unbeknownst to me, things had always been bad, but they had been getting far worse of late. The incidents of violence were more severe and coming more often to the point Sheryl simply couldn't put up with Greg anymore.

One night, Sheryl went out with some friends, including a man named Walt Rohr. At the end of the night, Walt gave her a ride home. When she came through the door, Greg was irate. He made her undress in front of him and went so far as to put his hands inside her vagina to "check" if she had been with anyone else sexually. He told her she had have sex with him immediately and if she didn't, it was proof she had been with Walt. As she had so many times before, Sheryl had sex with him so he wouldn't become even more furious.

On his birthday, July 6, Greg and Sheryl went out for dinner, then out to Jim's Tap afterwards. Several of Greg and Sheryl's friends were there. Sheryl sat at the bar with the other women while Greg sat at table with the men. Everyone was drinking and having a good time, at least ostensibly.

At around 9, Greg approached Sheryl at the bar and said he was ready to go home. Sheryl was still having a good time with her friends, so she told him she wanted to stay. Sheryl had to have known this would anger Greg. He was used to being treated like a king and here he was on his birthday, being blown off by his wife at the bar he went to three or four times a week, where everyone knew him.

This wasn't her normal style, not at all, she was always very submissive and did everything to keep Greg calm. But for whatever reason, she decided right then that this was the night she wasn't going to do it anymore.

This didn't go over well with Greg. He was surprised and quickly left in a huff. An hour later, he came back to collect Sheryl, whom he obviously considered to be his property. One can only imagine how angry he was. He walked up to the bar and interrupted Sheryl in the middle of her conversation and told her gruffly, "Let's go." This time she got up and left as she knew she had pushed him too far and she didn't want to cause a scene at the bar.

On the way home, Greg began to berate her. It started with him telling her that she was awful to him for not leaving the bar with him on his birthday, but as they drove, Greg began to list everything else that was wrong with her as well. It continued when they got home. Greg told her to sit down on the couch in the living room where he continued his verbal assault on her.

Finally, Sheryl said what she had been thinking for a long time. "I want out. I want a divorce. I can't take this anymore."

Greg looked at her for a second then said "Ok. Get out." He then reached over and grabbed her by her legs, pulling her off the couch. Sheryl was caught by surprise and her head hit the floor hard.

Of course, he didn't really want her to go. Even if she wanted to leave, he wouldn't have let her. Greg kept her up all night, not leaving her alone, harassing her and reprimanding her until she finally had sex with him. It was his birthday after all.

At my urging, Sheryl managed to convince Greg to go together to a marriage counselor, but it wasn't helpful. Sheryl told me the counselor told the two of them they were there too late. At the time, I didn't understand the comment. I still thought they could work things out.

I even thought for a while that things were better between them. They tried to spend some time together as family. Sheryl, Greg, and the boys went to Peoria and stayed overnight and went to the zoo. When I asked Sheryl how it went, all she said was that the boys had fun. Her silence about her own feelings were telling. When I talked with Lisa about the trip she was appalled because when Sheryl came back, she had hickeys all over her neck. Greg had marked her so everyone could see she was his property.

To no one's surprise, Greg wasn't handling this well. He was all over the place. On the one hand, he constantly begged Sheryl not to leave and told her how much he loved her. She told me often how much this behavior made her sick, how pathetic she thought it was. On the other hand, he often demanded that she leave, and he was the one who filed for divorce first, there was no way he was going to let her have that much control over this situation.

It was obvious almost immediately things would not go smoothly during this process. Greg swore if she left him, he would make sure she was ruined. He would get custody and she would never see the boys again; not if he could help it.

It was apparent she needed a lawyer who wasn't afraid to go to court and fight for custody; someone who is a real bulldog, which surprisingly isn't always easy to find.

I did my research and talked to my friend, Renee Monfort, who was a lawyer in Champaign, Illinois, and we both agreed Art Lerner was the best attorney for Sheryl. I set her up with Art. He was an old-school lawyer, one who had no problem battling it out in court. He was a bit irascible, had a hard time listening to his clients' concerns, and loved barking orders, but when it came down to it, he wasn't going to run from a fight. I sent her the 2,000 dollars for his retainer that I had managed to save.

Around this time, Sheryl was making some burgers on the grill when Greg came home. He had been drinking. She told him again they had to talk and that she wanted a divorce; that she was serious about it. When she was trying to turn the burgers over, he flipped the grill against the side of the garage, causing it to catch fire.

Sheryl screamed for him to put it out, but he said "No, let it burn." She ended up putting the fire out with a hose while Greg watched enraged.

While she may have been afraid of Greg, what she was really terrified of was the possibility that he was going to take her children. And the thing is, she was right to be worried.

If one is going into a custody battle, especially against someone as unhinged as Greg, everything has to be documented. I told Sheryl she had to write everything down, what he did, what he said, what he accused her of, all of it. She had to keep track of everything.

Once again, she dutifully complied with my request. She used a spiral notebook with Spiderman on the cover that was going to be used by her oldest boy for kindergarten and started writing everything down that went on between her and Greg. Much of what she wrote was written as if she was documenting a patient's chart at work but it all ended up being invaluable during the years of investigation of Greg and then at the murder trial 27 years later.

She began to take other steps to be on her own as well. She didn't have any credit cards or even any established credit, so she started applying for credit using our parents' address. She started to look at apartments to move into, ones that she could afford and were big enough for the children. She began looking at vehicles that got better gas mileage than her Blazer and she put a new bed on layaway.

Greg wasn't sitting idly by waiting to see what Sheryl would do. As soon as she told him she wanted a divorce, he ran out and got an attorney of his own, a very flamboyant man named Keith Hayes, whose appearance reminded me a little of Colonel Sanders.

Hayes didn't have a reputation for being a great attorney, but that wasn't necessarily a good thing for Sheryl. To fight against a bad attorney is often worse than going against the best attorney. The best attorney follows the rules and is rational. The bad attorney does the same thing as bad people do and acts like the law doesn't apply to them. As much as it pains me to say it, the court system doesn't always work. If someone lies and won't follow the rules, they just might win. It often rewards people like Greg, those that have no conscience or moral code.

Hayes even made house calls. As the days went on and things became more volatile and the cops were called, Hayes would show up on the scene.

Sheryl was shocked when Greg filed for divorce, since he was begging her to stay. Art advised her to file her own petition as well, that way she had something going herself if Greg decided not to follow through.

There was nothing Greg wouldn't stoop to; he tried every dirty trick in the book. He made a report to the Department of Children and Family Services claiming that Sheryl was abusive and an unfit mother. Of course, this was beyond ridiculous. Still, they had to do their due diligence and started an investigation, including home visits and interviewing the boys and my parents. Greg lied about everything. Sheryl was terrified.

Greg took pictures of every scratch and bruise any of the boys had, to use against her in court, saying that Sheryl had been abusing the children. And there were plenty of those. These kids weren't playing video games all day, they played outside most of the day and they played rough.

He even tried to turn her in for using drugs when he found a few of my mother's muscle relaxers in her purse. He accused her of being an alcoholic, even though she barely drank.

And it went on. He accused her of infidelity, saying she was having an affair with Walt. I was sure that this was just more gaslighting by Greg.

One night, things exploded. Greg wouldn't leave Sheryl alone and followed her all around the house, getting in her face, threatening her, and getting physical. He forced her down on the floor in the basement, held her down by her arms, and bit her breasts, trying to force himself on her.

While on her back, fighting him off, Sheryl scratched him in self-defense and, amazingly, Greg called the police on her because he felt he had injuries he could show the arriving officer to prove how insane she was. This didn't work out quite the way he thought. A deputy came to the house and Greg was arrested on a charge of battery. Greg truly had no shame, after he attacked her, he filed for an emergency order of protection from Sheryl. She followed suit with one of her own.

Greg quickly bailed out of jail. It wasn't a serious charge and if found guilty, he probably would have just received a slap on the wrist, but as things turned out, we will never know because Sheryl wasn't around to testify against him. As always, Greg doubled down. Along with the order of protection against Sheryl, his attorney suggested he always have Les or another one of his friends with him when anything was going on with him and Sheryl in the future, so he could have a witness against her if anything else happened.

After Greg was arrested for battery Sheryl told me she knew something about him that would put him away for a long time if she decided to tell it. I never asked what it was. I will always regret that. At the time, I just didn't want to know. I suspected drug activity or that Greg had illegitimate children, but later believed that he probably did something much worse like raped or killed someone else.

This idea didn't come out of nowhere. There was a well-publicized rape of a young woman who was jogging on Sheryl's road not too far from her house not too long before Sheryl was killed. As the woman was jogging, a man came out of a cornfield and grabbed her, held her down, and raped her. She couldn't identify her rapist but was able to give enough of a description that a composite sketch was drawn and circulated. I always thought that drawing strongly resembled Greg.

Greg used this rape later to frighten Sheryl, saying he thought he had seen a prowler in the cornfield near their home, and that she should be careful. He might have been just gaslighting her, but it's possible he was trying to set up an alibi.

For the first time, I knew for a fact she was being abused. It wasn't just her being yelled at or him making threats. He wasn't just a jerk. He was physically hurting my sister.

When I asked her if she was afraid of him, and I did this often, she would always say, "I can handle him." But could she? He knew she wanted out, and not only that, but other people were also now involved. Whatever Greg had been up to, all of the dark, violent things he was doing, if Sheryl decided to talk, he could be found out. Everyone might find out the truth about Greg Houser.

Things started to fall apart rapidly. Sheryl and I talked daily, and she gave me permission to communicate directly with her attorney to help her stay on top of each new development.

We became closer than ever as the days went on. One by one, she started to reveal the secrets she had kept for so many years. She began to confide in me more than ever and slowly began to answer my questions openly. I always suspected Greg may have pushed her around as I had witnessed a lot of verbal abuse over the years. but I had no idea of the torture he was truly capable of.

After everything that had gone on, she could no longer deny the abuse. She started to tell me in bits and pieces about what she had suffered for the seven years of their marriage. I asked her if he had abused the boys. She denied it but did so in the exact same way that she initially denied he abused her. That frightened me to death. She would say "He can do whatever he wants to me, but I am not going to let him hurt my babies."

I had heard Greg berate the boys and call them sissies when they cried. One day, after I asked her the question for at least the tenth time, she told me that once Greg spanked the oldest boy so hard for getting out of bed to get a drink of water that he wet the bed.

Even worse, one afternoon she came home and found Greg in the kitchen with the oldest boy. Greg had his arms and legs duct taped to a chair. Greg's reason for this was that the oldest boy wasn't behaving.

I knew the kids were terrified of him. If he barked at them, they would act like little soldiers, they dared not disobey. It wasn't uncommon for him to grab their arms and jerk them around or tell them to shut up.

As we talked, it came out Greg had been abusing her since they dated. In the beginning, the abuse was not so bad and didn't happen often. She could tolerate it and for the most part didn't even recognize it for what it was. But as time went on the attacks got worse and came closer and closer together.

This was mindboggling to me. I asked her why she married him if he was so awful to her. She responded she didn't think she would find anyone else who would marry her and all she ever wanted was to get married and have babies. I asked her why she had three children when things were so bad between them and she said, "He was always nice to me when I was pregnant." Hearing these things broke my heart.

Most of the abuse was sexual and involved him choking her with his hands or ropes. If Greg didn't get sex every day, he became very aggressive and nasty. She used to hate going to bed so much she would stay up late and clean the house even though she had to get up early in the morning for work. She never minded when Greg got really drunk because that meant he might pass out before she went to bed and she would be spared, at least for one night.

There were other things that were very typical of a woman in a relationship with an abuser. Greg controlled her every move. Greg wouldn't let her wear makeup. She had to have supper on the table at 5 or he would get extremely angry. She wasn't free to visit family and friends and we certainly knew we weren't welcome at their home if he was there. The list went on.

Things continued to spiral out of control. One day Greg would beg her to come back to him, forget the past and start anew, the next he would push her outside and lock the door when it was her turn to take the kids. How was she supposed to forget the past when he did something awful with each new day?

Sheryl found a loaded gun hidden in a closet. Greg always had guns, but they were always where Sheryl knew they would be, not hidden away in a place she didn't know about. After finding the hidden weapon, Sheryl was afraid to stay at home alone so she asked our father to stay with her. When Greg came home and asked why he was there, Sheryl said it was because she was scared.

Greg would never actually confront my father and was always a little intimidated by him. My father was mellow and easygoing. He had a long fuse, but when it went off, you better look out. His years of working on the farm made him no one to be messed with. Greg didn't want any part of him.

Greg left the house in a rage saying he was going to call the sheriff about this situation. Soon he came back with Les Shores because his attorney said to have a witness in all situations such as this. The police came back and told Greg there was nothing they could do.

One morning, Sheryl was in the bathroom brushing her teeth wearing her nightgown. Greg came into the bathroom and shut the door asking if they could talk.

He started off by saying, "If we have to live together, couldn't we just be nice to each other and get along while we do?" Sheryl said yes, they could certainly try and then went into the bedroom to get dressed.

Greg followed and told her he needed her for just two minutes so he could prove something to her, holding up two fingers as he did so. He then told her to lie on the bed. Sheryl had a good idea of what he wanted to prove and said "No!" as forcefully as she could.

Greg told her then he had taken a photo of the boys when they had bruises on them, and he would tell the court she was a child abuser and have them taken away from her if she wasn't nicer to him. He told her again to lie on the bed.

What follows is from Sheryl's journal.

> *"I lay down on the bed, I was crying and telling him "No"! He told me to stop crying, he got up and shut the bedroom door, I could hear the boys awake in their room, the baby was crying. He came to me and took off my underwear, I still had my bra on. He started having oral sex with me, licking my genitals. I had my hands across my chest, he told me to move them, I said No! I was crying, I turned over to get away from him., he turned me back over and tried again, I was screaming. He*

kept threatening to take the boys from me. I was sitting on the side of the bed, he was standing in front of me, told me quit crying and said he didn't hurt me. He took down his shorts and put his penis in my face and told me to suck on it. He took the back of my head and pushed my mouth on it, told me to keep sucking and do a good job or I would be sorry. I did this four times then stopped. He got really mad; I could see it in his eyes. He told me I didn't do a good enough job and I would be sorry."

When he was done assaulting her sexually, Greg got dressed and left for work, peeling out in the driveway as he did so often.

Sheryl was distraught and cried all the way to work. Later that day, she worked up her courage and called Art Lerner and told him about the sexual assault she suffered. He said to go to the courthouse immediately and get another order of protection. Amazingly, the court ruled Greg could still live in the house with her, he just couldn't "harass" her. Times certainly were different then.

During this time, the boys were spending more time at our parents' house. They seemed okay considering the situation and didn't ask about Greg very much. It wasn't that Greg wanted the children, he could care less about being a good father, he just didn't want Sheryl to have them.

One day, she took the boys out to lunch at Hardees and the oldest said, "Mommy you hurt my feelings." When Sheryl asked him why, he had tears in his eyes and said, "Because you and Daddy fight." She asked him if it would be better if Mommy and Daddy didn't live together anymore and he said yes, it would. Sheryl's oldest told her that he didn't want to go back to the house until Daddy was gone.

He was unconscionable. Greg would say things in front of the children about how if Sheryl didn't come back to him things would get a lot worse, that he hadn't done anything to her yet, but if she didn't start to straighten up, he very well might. He told the boys he would take them away from her. He would ask Sheryl in front of them why she didn't care about their three little boys.

The abuse continued to escalate. One night he put his hands around her throat and squeezed until she couldn't breathe. He looked her in the eye and said, "If I ever catch you with another man, I will blow you and him away." Then he pointed a finger at her and made a sound like a gun going off.

In late August, Sheryl got some good news. The Department of Child and Family Services finished its investigation and found all of Greg's reports unfounded. The caseworker from DCFS not only found in Sheryl's favor but she was so concerned about Sheryl's safety that she told her she needed to talk to her lawyer about a better order of protection and she gave her the contact for the local woman's shelter. Since both Sheryl and Greg had been granted separate orders of protection against the other and the court had done nothing more than tell them not to harass each other, Art Lerner drafted a motion for temporary custody and filed it with the court.

At the hearing on Sheryl's motion for temporary custody, a settlement was reached by Sheryl and Greg's respective attorneys that Greg and Sheryl would share custody of the kids who would reside full time in the home and Greg and Sheryl would rotate in and out every 3 ½ days. Today, no judge would ever enter such a ridiculous order in an abuse case such as this. Even back then though I thought it was the stupidest thing I had ever heard. Our only hope was this would soon be over.

But it wasn't. On September 2, Sheryl went to her house after work only to find Greg had put a deadbolt lock on the back door and chain locks on the front and side door.

Sheryl couldn't believe it. She went to the side door and opened the lock with her key, but it wouldn't open all the way with the chain on it. While Sheryl wasn't a violent or angry person, this made her furious. She crashed into the door three times with her shoulder and got inside the house. She took her mail and went back to our parents' house where she was staying.

It wasn't long before Greg called and threatened her, saying she had broken a lock and if she didn't come talk to him right away, then she was in big trouble. Sheryl went back to the house with a Piatt County Sheriff's Office deputy. While there, Greg continually asked her to be arrested for breaking into his home saying things like, "Will justice ever be served?" Upon the deputy discovering that Sheryl's name was on the deed to the house, too, he conceded to Greg that there was nothing he could do.

A few days after the "break in," Greg told Sheryl, "You will be sorry if you don't come back. I will fight to the end and I will win."

THREE

Sept. 20, 1990, was a Thursday. At 8:20 a.m., Greg called Sheryl while she was at work.

He was more polite than usual, pleasant even. As it was his turn to take care of the children and she hadn't seen them for a few days, Sheryl asked him how the boys were. He said they were fine. He went on to say that last night he and Tim Byrd were hanging out at the house playing pool and drinking beer in the garage when around midnight they heard a person out in the cornfield.

Sheryl wasn't sure why he told her this, so she told him it wasn't her. Greg said he knew it wasn't and he just wanted her to know so she would be careful when she was there, alone in the house.

He asked Sheryl if she might want to go out and eat supper with him and the boys. She said she didn't know if that was a good idea or not.

He seemed to accept that but said he wanted her to come to the house after work and see the boys because they had been asking about her and missed her. He also wanted her to check on the baby. He had a runny nose and a cough and was not feeling well. He had asthma which was triggered by viruses. Sheryl knew he was sick and worried about him because he often needed nebulizer treatments if the virus triggered his asthma and Greg was not accustomed to giving him these treatments. Sheryl said she would come after work if he told her when a good time would be to say hi to the boys and check on the baby. Greg said he wouldn't be home until around 4:30. Sheryl said she would be come by then but couldn't stay long.

At around 4:30, Sheryl called and told him she would be working late until 7:30 or 8 because they were really busy, so she wouldn't come by because by then it would too late. He said no, it would be great if she still came. The boys really wanted to see her so he would keep them up until she got there. Sheryl, with her mothering instincts hard to deny, said she would.

At 8, she called Greg back and told him she still hadn't left work yet and it would be at least another hour. She told him not to keep the boys up, because it would be too late. He said he would put the oldest and the youngest to bed but the middle one, who was the "night owl" was wound up and he would let him stay up so she could see him. Greg also still wanted her to check the baby and make sure he was okay. Sheryl said no, it would be too late, but Greg insisted, insinuating Sheryl didn't care about the boys enough to come and check on them. Sheryl, partly worried about the boys, and partly worried about what Greg might say to the court if she gave him any ammunition, told him she would stop by, but just for a few minutes.

She didn't get to the house until around 9:45. The house looked dark except for a light or two, and there were no outside lights on. When Sheryl got out of the car, she left her car running.

She knocked once on the back door, but no one came. She tried the knob. It was unlocked so she went in. For a moment, she hesitated at the top of the steps leading to the basement as the laundry room lights were on, but the rest of the house was dark.

Sheryl went up into the kitchen and into the boy's bedroom, but there was no sign of Greg. She checked on the boys, all were sleeping soundly.

And then, he was there. Greg stood behind her in the room.

He said, "Be quiet! They're all asleep." Sheryl could smell whiskey on his breath.

He told Sheryl to come in the dining room and sit down. Sheryl said she would, but just for a moment. She sat in a recliner while he sat at the table. Almost immediately he started in again, asking why they couldn't get back together, and if it was really over.

The baby woke up and started crying. Sheryl went in to pick him up while Greg went downstairs to check on his laundry. When Greg came back upstairs, he told Sheryl to go outside to shut her car off while he held the baby. Sheryl did so, then came back in and laid him back in his crib and rubbed his back so he would go to sleep.

Once the baby was sleeping soundly, Sheryl told Greg she had to leave. She was really tired and had to work tomorrow. He asked her to give him just a minute and wanted her to come into the dining room and talk to him because they had to set up some rules if he was going to let her see the boys when it was his turn to have them. Despite her better judgement, she decided to talk to him; the boys were her weakness and for once Greg was being at least somewhat nice.

Then he started in again and asked her why it had to be over. Why did she have to leave him? Then he wanted to know why she never called him when she had the boys. The answer to this, of course, was that she couldn't stand him, and was afraid of him, but she obviously didn't tell him that.

They weren't getting anywhere talking. It was the same old conversation they had had numerous times. Sheryl told him once again she was tired and had to work tomorrow. She had to go.

Sheryl stood up to leave but Greg said, "Come here."
She said, "No."

He stood up and grabbed her jacket with both hands and said, "You aren't going anywhere."

Sheryl had seen a lot of darkness in the man she chose to marry. She had been witness to Greg doing a lot of terrible things and she had seen the depths of his anger hundreds of times, but when she looked in his eyes, she saw something different than she ever had before. And what she saw scared her.

Greg said, "You're coming with me."

Sheryl said, "No, please don't hurt me."

He began to drag her into the bedroom.

She started screaming, "Help me!" She screamed harder when she saw there was a rope tied to the headboard of the bed.

He put his hand in her mouth to gag her and told her to shut up and that she better not scream. He threw her down on the bed on her back and sat on her legs and abdomen. She screamed again. That's when he put the sheets from the bed in her mouth to gag her.

What happened next is best told in Sheryl's own words from her journal.[1]

> *"I was really scared. I thought I was going to die. He held my hands above my head. He had a rope tied to the bed and he tied it around one of my wrists. I started fighting him. We rolled on the bed. I tried to get him off me. I couldn't. I started kicking and biting and scratching him, but I couldn't get him off. He kept gagging me with the sheets and putting his hand over my face and trying to suffocate me. He put my head down in the bed trying to suffocate me. He got me back on my back and sat on top of me, he told me to put my hands above my head and to keep them there and*

---

1. All grammar, spelling and punctuation errors are due to the original author.

not to move them. I did what he said. I was scared, I thought what could I do, so I calmed down and started talking to him, trying to back him down. He had put the rope around my neck at one point and I managed to get it off. He pulled down his pants and put his hard penis in my face and told me to suck on it. I did it two times and he said "again" really hard., I didn't want to. He took the rope and put it in my mouth and held my head down with it with one hand. With the other hand he pulled my sweatshirt up and undid my bra and unzipped my pants. He put his hand in my vagina and said, "I'm going to get you all lubed up." Then he started sucking on my breasts, he did each one a couple of times. He still had the rope across my mouth. He said if I can't have you no one can, I'm going to make you confess to being with Walt. The sweat was dripping off him and on to me."

Sheryl began trying to calm him down. As she wrote:

I put my hands on his face and started talking to him, look what you are doing? You're hurting me, look what you're doing to us. He said "No. Look what you're doing to us. I just kept talking to him until I got him talked into getting off of me. He let me stand at the side of the bed."

Once free, she started to put her pants on, but Greg told her to stop and stood in front of the bedroom door so she couldn't leave. Apparently, Greg had a plan, albeit a rather inane one, that would allow him to get away with sexually assaulting her. He pulled out a blank piece of paper and a pen and told her to write "I consent to having sex with you" and sign her name to it. Sheryl refused.

After what seemed like hours, Greg finally let her out the bedroom door, but her nightmare wasn't over. As soon as she got out, she ran as fast as she could to the front door. She managed to get the chain lock off and the door unlocked, but Greg grabbed her when was almost out, pulled her back, and dragged her into the living room.

She started yelling the oldest boy's name as loudly as she could. Of course, he wouldn't be able to help but Sheryl thought Greg wouldn't do anything to her with her children watching. Greg put his hand in her mouth to gag her again and told her to shut up.

He bent her over the back of the couch and put the paper and pen in front of her and once again told her to write "I consent to have sex with you" and to sign her name. Once more Sheryl refused.

Finally, he let her up. Sheryl begged him to let her go as her parents would be looking for her. She was already late home from work, they would be worried.

Greg let her go again and she ran to the back door. He followed, grabbed her again, and put his hand on the door. He made her promise she wouldn't call the police and turn him in before he let her go.

Sheryl said she wouldn't tell the police. What else would she say at that moment?

Greg let her go and she ran to her neighbors' house, Chris and Jackie, who lived in a trailer about a quarter of a mile away. Hysterical, Sheryl banged on the door. She told them to call the police, she had no interest in keeping up her side of the deal with her monstrous soon-to-be-ex-husband.

When the police arrived, they questioned Sheryl, then went to the house to arrest Greg.

He was charged with one count of aggravated criminal sexual assault, a Class X Felony; two counts of criminal sexual assault, a Class I Felony; and one count of unlawful restraint. He bailed out once again. But this time was different. There wouldn't be just a little slap on the wrist for Greg this time. Because of his predatory, violent personality and sheer stupidity, if he was convicted as charged, he was going to prison. Maybe for a long time.

The following day, Sheryl filed a petition for emergency relief and temporary custody hearing. Four days after the aggravated criminal sexual assault, the judge heard Sheryl's petition for emergency relief, revoked the temporary custody order previously entered by the court, and awarded Sheryl the temporary care, custody, and control of the children along with house. Greg was granted three hours a week of supervised visitation by DCFS. Sheryl was told to box Greg's clothes to be picked up by him. Greg moved in with his parents.

On September 28 and October 3, Greg and Sheryl underwent polygraph tests regarding the aggravated attempted sexual assault. Greg's results were erratic and inconsistent on the events of that night which precluded the examiner from rendering a definite opinion. On the other hand, Sheryl's responses showed no emotional response indicative of deception regarding the events of that night.

As awful as this was, there was a silver lining. She had it made. It was all over now. Greg didn't have a leg to stand on when it came to the impending divorce and custody arrangements.

But one day, a few days after the sexual assault, Sheryl told me for the first time she was really scared. She saw the look in his eye that night and knew he really could kill her. When he let her go that night, he thought he owned her, that she was cowed, and she would never tell what he did to her. And she told a lot and was prepared to tell it all.

The next day, I called Art Lerner on the phone to talk about the newest developments in the case. I could tell he was concerned but I don't think he was quite grasping my fears. As we ended the call, I said, "You may think I am saying this because I am Sheryl's sister and this is my heart talking, but I am telling you this because I really fear this might happen. He is going to kill her."

Sheryl told me often that she was thinking of dropping the aggravated sexual assault charge. I explained it wasn't her choice. It was a criminal case so the State had control of that decision, but if she refused to testify, they probably wouldn't pursue the charges as they would have no case. Greg begged her not to cooperate with the State's Attorney, using his typical back and forth psycho personality of going from being nice to threatening her.

On September 26, 1990, Art wrote Sheryl a letter telling her that he would work on getting her child support but to sit tight because Greg would be busy with the criminal case. He advised her that he can't use the criminal case against Greg to gain an advantage in the divorce, he'll answer her questions but he wanted her to work closely with Roger. The last sentence of his letter he wrote, "I want you to be very careful, because I believe that your former husband has a "get even" personality. He will be attempting in any way possible, to blacken your name through the claim of drug use, alcohol use, or failing to care for the children."

FOUR

When I saw John in the door of my office, I screamed. My boss, Lester, ran into the room and stared at me in shock. I continued to scream, "He killed her! He killed her! I told you he was going to kill her!" Pain and grief surged through my body.

Seeing Lester caused my mind to shift briefly. I told him I had just finished a call with another attorney, and we had finally reached a settlement in a case that had been dragging on forever. I began to explain the terms of the settlement and told him I could draft it up before I went home so the case wouldn't continue to linger.

He looked at me like I was out of my mind and said, "Renee. Stop, just go, I've got this under control!"

John ushered me out of the office, through the halls and down the grand staircase through the lobby and into the parking lot. Everyone froze and stared as we walked past. Some knew about my sister's situation and guessed what had happened that caused such a violent reaction from me while others must have thought I had lost my mind.

We got in John's car and spent the next hour in silence as we drove back to our condo. I wanted to know the details of what had happened, who had the kids, whether Greg had been arrested, and how my family was and what they were doing. John didn't know the answers to any of my questions so there was nothing to talk about.

Once we got home, I immediately called Lisa and asked her what happened. She told me when Sheryl didn't show up to work they called her home and the oldest boy answered the phone. He first said he couldn't find her, then said she was asleep with a rope around her neck and he couldn't wake her up. At this, 911 was called. I wanted to know if Greg had been arrested. He had not. Then I asked whether Mom had the boys, which she did not. While I couldn't imagine why Greg had not been arrested, the first order of business was to take care of the boys so I assumed my role as the problem solver and told Lisa to get the boys and hide them until I could get home and figure out what to do.

I had failed Sheryl. I wasn't going to further let her down and let him get the boys.

I began making phone calls to arrange a flight right away. I had never booked a flight the same day I was to fly but I knew it would be expensive. I heard that some airlines had bereavement rates so I looked into those. I was still a new lawyer. I had a large amount of student loan debt and virtually no extra money as I had just loaned what I had saved to Sheryl for a retainer to hire Art. Even with the bereavement rate, the tickets were still $900 each.

I thought to myself, "Oh my god, that son-of-a-bitch just murdered my sister and now I have to spend $1,800 I don't have to go to her funeral."

I vowed at that moment to never let Greg Houser have the satisfaction of ruining my life. Rather, I told myself then, and repeated to myself many times since then, that Greg Houser may have changed my life when he murdered my sister but I would never give him the satisfaction of ruining it.

After I secured tickets, I went into my home office, looked through the bills and other things that were going to need to be done in the immediate future. I had to make sure none of our bills went past due while we were away and that our affairs were in order. I couldn't imagine leaving without doing so. I called our downstairs neighbors, let them know what had happened and that we were leaving, and wondered if they could collect our mail and watch our place. John was irritated with me and kept hurrying me along saying, "Come on, come on, let's go!" That was easy for him to say but I had to take care of business and I still had to pack.

I stared at the clothes in my closet trying to figure out what I was going to wear to my sister's funeral. It was important to me that I pick just the right outfit. I selected a muted green floral skirt with a cream blouse and a hunter green blazer. These were the first really nice professional articles of clothing that I had been able to afford. I was proud of that outfit, liked the way it looked on me, and thought that Sheryl would have thought I looked very professional in it.

At the time, I didn't even think about the possibility of Greg getting away with killing her. That thought never occurred to me. How could it? Everyone knew he did it. While Greg hadn't yet been arrested when I talked to Lisa, in my mind I assumed he would be in jail by the time I got home later that day. There was no way he would still be out walking around. It was so obvious he killed her. We would be dealing with a court case, and possibly a trial and that wouldn't be easy on my family.

I never thought he would walk free for the next 27 years.

I found out later, that on that fateful day, my father was working in the field when he saw a friend, Billy, walking towards him, approaching his combine. Billy told him that something had happened at Sheryl's house and he needed to get my mom and go check on her. My father immediately left the field and went to the nursing home where my mother worked and told her they needed to go to Sheryl's house right away. My mom was passing meds and unbeknownst to her, the rest of the staff had already heard that an emergency call had come in dispatching emergency vehicles to Sheryl's house. When my dad arrived, my mom told him she couldn't go because she was passing out meds. Her boss knew what had been going on with Sheryl and told my mom, "Go, go, we'll pass meds, just go." She left with my dad.

They went straight to the boys' babysitter's house. Her name was Mrs. Mackey. They knew Sheryl should be at work and the boys would be there. Mrs. Mackey, like everyone else, already knew. When my mom knocked on the door, Mrs. Mackey was obviously shaken and nervous and told my parents that, "she didn't bring the boys today and you need to go out to the house."

When my parents got close to Sheryl's home and saw EMT vehicles and police cars at her house, their hearts raced. Neither one dared to say a word, too afraid that if they said what they were thinking—the worst thing that could have happened— might be true. They got out of the car and began to run into the garage where people were gathered to see what was going on when they were stopped by a police officer who told them Sheryl was dead. She was found hanging by a rope around her neck in the garage.

My parents instantly knew that Greg did this to her. They began crying and begging to see her. They wanted to help her. They knew that if all these people would get out of their way and let them see her, they could help her. They knew that these people were wrong and she wasn't really dead. She couldn't be dead. She was only 29 and had three small boys to raise.

They stood in front of our car, held each other, and cried. It was as if the moment wasn't real. Chris Doenitz, who lived down the road, approached them and told them how sorry he was, trying to ease their pain. My parents started to realize this wasn't just a bad dream. Chris told them that the three boys were okay and that they were with his wife, Jackie, at their house. My parents were relieved that their grandchildren were alive and safe, but thoughts of horror went through their heads knowing their beautiful daughter was really dead. What would happen to those three little boys now?

It's interesting how Greg didn't wind up with the boys that day. Because he was there. For some odd reason, he was at the fire station washing his truck when the call came in that something was going on at Sheryl's house that needed emergency attention. When he got to the house, Greg didn't attempt to console the boys or even check on them and make sure they were okay. He just asked the first responders at the scene, "What has Sheryl done now?" So Jackie took it upon herself to take the boys home with her and make sure they were safe.

Jackie called my Aunt Kathy saying that she was scared that Greg would come and take the boys and she wanted someone to get them. Aunt Kathy and her husband George both worked in pediatric social services. Sheryl and I had talked to them during the course of the divorce as they were a wealth of information and supportive of Sheryl and our family. Lisa had a friend who was a social worker who also tried to help that day and she was vehemently opposed to any of us taking the boys without a court order. Thank God, Aunt Kathy and Uncle George ignored Lisa's friend and picked the boys up from Jackie and took them to my Uncle Jim's and Aunt Bonnie's to hide.

On the way to Uncle Jim and Aunt Bonnie's house, they stopped and picked up my grandfather, Walter, who brought along his shotgun. Grandpa was determined to hunt Greg down and kill him. He said that he was old and if he went to jail, he didn't care, and then they could pay for all of his expensive medicine.

The boys were fed dinner. The oldest picked up the baby, turned him upside down and tried to smash his head on the ground. Aunt Kathy took the oldest back to a bedroom to calm him down and talk to him. All he could do was shake. He wasn't able to speak. Aunt Kathy was sure he was acting out something he had seen. The boys were put to bed.

Shortly after that, DeWitt County Deputies came to the door and said that they were patrolling the area but given the woods behind the house they didn't know if they could protect everyone. They suggested that the children be moved out of county with their escort and that no one be told where they were taken.

My family was shattered. We wanted to help her. We wanted what every family wants for one of their own—safety and happiness. We wanted the violence to stop but we just didn't know how to make that happen. She had a good attorney, support from her family and friends, and had recently gotten sole temporary custody. My parents watched the boys every chance they could to help her out and to keep some stability and happiness in their lives. My father stayed with her at her house and even offered her a gun at one point but she wouldn't take it. She didn't want one in the house with the children. The violence kept increasing but my family didn't know what else to do. We felt so helpless. We thought that after she was granted custody of the children and possession of the home and Greg received supervised visitation that it would soon be over and she and the boys could go on with their lives. What we understand now, but didn't then, was that that was when she was in the most danger.

We have often asked ourselves if there was something more or different that we could have done for Sheryl that would have resulted in a different ending. It's a horrible thing to live with.

But when John and I flew out of Orlando, I knew none of this. Because we got tickets at the last minute, we were not able to sit next to each other, so I sat by myself with tears openly streaming down my face. I tried, but I couldn't stop them from coming. A woman sitting next to me kindly asked me if I was ok. I replied, "I'm on my way home because my sister was murdered by her husband last night." She never said another word to me the rest of the way.

When we got to my parents' house, there was a huge crowd of people there. It was a small town, one where after a tragedy, neighbors still brought food over, visited, and helped in any way they could. My best friend from high school was there waiting for me. It was nice to see a familiar, caring face.

As much as people were attempting to be kind, it was still shocking to be confronted by all these people in the kitchen before I even had a chance to see my parents or my sisters or process anything. I ran upstairs to try and get away from everyone for just a few minutes and talk to Lisa. I had so many questions. I wanted to know exactly what she knew, how she found out, who had the boys, and whether Greg had been arrested which I totally expected by the time I got home. Seeing my parents broke my heart. My mom was despondent and it was the first time I ever recall seeing my dad cry. Just seeing that made me cry even harder.

After everyone left, it was even worse. We were terrified he was outside the house watching us. My mom and dad went to bed and myself, John, Lisa and her husband, and Julie and her husband, all grabbed sleeping bags and slept on the living room floor together. At one point, we saw a flicker of light and thought it was him with a flashlight stalking us until we realized it was just a spark from the electric fence.

Although one may think our feelings were an overreaction, they were based on reality. Exactly what I feared would happen, happened—my sister was dead at Greg's hands. For weeks after Sheryl's death, our friends and family worked out a schedule where someone came at 10:00 p.m. every night to our house and sat guard at the kitchen table near the back door with a gun so we could try to sleep. In my mind, these folks were not just protecting us from Greg but protecting Greg from us. I seriously thought that my dad may try to leave the house, hunt Greg down, and kill him just like he had killed Sheryl. As much as the thought brought satisfaction, I knew that the boys needed my dad now more than ever, so to have him in prison would not do any of us any good.

The next day, we found out that the judge had entered an order in the divorce case directing the Illinois Department of Children and Family Services to take custody of the children and place them with my parents. The day of October 5, 1990, was chaotic and crazy, but at least we had the boys and weren't going to let anything happen to them. Unbeknownst to us, on October 5th, the day Sheryl was found dead, Greg's attorney filed a motion on Greg's behalf to dismiss the divorce case since Sheryl had died. If the judge granted the motion, the order granting Sheryl temporary custody would not have been in effect and the boys would have reverted to Greg automatically.

I'm grateful to this day that the judge did not dismiss the divorce case because if he had, things would have been very different. In 1990 in Illinois, grandparents didn't have standing, or the right to seek custody of their grandchildren if a parent were alive and wanted them, so my parents wouldn't have even had the right to seek custody.

It wasn't long before we found out why Greg was walking around free after killing Sheryl. Some people thought it was suicide, as there was a ladder found next to her body where she was hung from a pipe. While I wasn't surprised that Greg's family was contending she committed suicide, I couldn't fathom anyone else had that thought. Greg's family had already proven that they were going to defend their baby boy to the bitter end. They denied any abuse of Sheryl by Greg. They were gaslighting right along with Greg. Sheryl had postpartum depression after she gave birth to her third baby boy because she so desperately wanted a girl.

None of us could believe it. Were these people so foolish? She didn't commit suicide. He killed her. How could people be so stupid? This wasn't a murder committed by a criminal mastermind, it was done by Greg.

The bizarre nightmare had started. He wasn't going to be arrested? He just tried to kill her two weeks ago and now he actually had done it and he still was walking around free?

At my first opportunity, I called Art Lerner and bluntly said, "I told you it was going to happen, now what do we do?" I suppose I could have been kinder to Art, it certainly wasn't his fault, but at this point I wasn't much in the mood to consider his feelings.

Art said we needed to do a custody order immediately to protect the children. Grandparents didn't even have the right to ask for custody if there was a living parent. They would have to prove that Greg was unfit. Of course, he was unfit. He murdered his children's mother after all. But if he wasn't going to be arrested and tried for her murder, we were left to fight to prove in a civil court that he was unfit. There was no choice. He had killed Sheryl and her boys couldn't be left to be tortured by this monster.

While the boys were our number one priority, we had other things to be worried about. At this point we weren't just concerned about the kids' safety; we were concerned for all of our safety also. It wasn't just us that was afraid of him either. Jackie and Chris were too. That is why they insisted we get the boys from them. They had their own children to protect and keeping the boys made them a target.

We were terrified. We knew someone intimately who not only was a killer, but who had killed my sister. Who was to say the boys wouldn't be next? Who is to say I wouldn't be? It wasn't like he thought much of me and what I stood for. If he could kill my sister in cold blood, who else might he kill?

We were afraid of him, but even more so, we were afraid of what he might do to the children to punish us. One might think we were being paranoid, but were we? Greg was a cold-blooded, psychopathic murderer.

My grandfather was fixated on killing Greg but my Aunt Kathy persuaded him to stay with the boys and protect them. She genuinely wanted the security of her father and his shotgun around, but more importantly, he needed to be given a purpose to keep him from hunting Greg down and killing him. While we all might have felt some satisfaction with that result, we all knew in the end it wouldn't serve any of us well.

The next day, we started the process of making funeral arrangements. My parents were in shock, so it was my sisters and I who took care of all the logistics. We all went to the funeral home together. When I walked into the funeral home and saw the casket, I immediately became enraged and screamed, "That fucking son of my bitch murdered my sister."

You could have heard a pin drop on the carpet. I'll never forget the stunned look on the funeral home director's face.

I was so shaken seeing her lifeless body lying in a casket in that dreary funeral home parlor that I couldn't think. The funeral home director began asking me simple questions like the middle names of the boys and I couldn't think of them.

Sheryl wanted to take her name back before her death so there was no way I was going to allow the name Houser to appear in her obituary and no Housers were to be allowed at the visitation. I'm confident that after my outburst when I walked in, the funeral director knew he would have to keep the Houser family away from me. I was never sure if he let them in when we weren't around.

In writing this book, I came across a note in Greg's handwriting signed by him and a witness that said, "I Greg Houser, give permission for the funeral home to embalm and prepare the body of Sheryl A. Houser. I am giving this permission only with the understanding and assurance that Phyllis and Victor Fehr are accepting complete and whole responsibility for all costs incurred relating to the death and burial of Sheryl A. Houser." The rage I experienced in the funeral home all those years ago returned. He claimed after her death that he still loved her, never wanted the divorce, and he felt so bad she was depressed enough to take her own life. What a disgusting person.

My mom was very traditional so there was no doubt there was going to be an open casket. The funeral director said if we wanted to do that, we needed to bring a turtleneck to cover Sheryl's wounds which caused me to lose it all over again.

We didn't have access to Sheryl's house to get clothing because it was a crime scene so we went to a little boutique in town called "Love's." Everyone in the store stopped and stared at us. They knew what had happened and why we were there. I couldn't stand the thought of having to pick out my sister's outfit for her own service. Turtlenecks were limited to a small section on the sale rack. A pretty green sweater caught my eye. We quickly agreed on it, paid for it, and left.

During visiting hours, I stood in line next to my parents, who were closest to the casket; we stood oldest to youngest. We shook hands and accepted condolences and hugs for hours. The line was out the door. No one asked us what happened or offered an opinion, but the looks I exchanged with nearly everyone I hugged assured me that everyone knew Greg killed Sheryl.

Art came through the line with his partner, Bob. Art extended his hand to me. I took it, drew him close to me, looked him in the eyes, and hissed, "I told you he was going to kill her and you didn't believe me." Even though I knew that there was nothing he could have done, I wanted him to feel bad.

After consulting with professionals, we opted not to bring any of the boys to any services for their mother. My mom took pictures of Sheryl in the casket because she thought it might be something the boys would want to look at someday. I was appalled at the thought and wanted to vomit.

It was so hard to keep it together. It lasted for hours. It was after 10 before we finally left.

The funeral was the following day at the Catholic church in Mahomet. That was the church she attended and we were afraid our home parish in Farmer City would be too small.

We were right. The church in Mahomet was packed. I stood at the back of the church before we paraded down the aisle following her casket trying to take in everyone who was in attendance. I interned at the Small Business Development Center and was shocked to see my boss from there in the pews. I have vivid memories of so many of the people who came through the line at the visitation and I saw at the funeral that I now make it a point to attend services for my co-workers, staff, family, and friends. I'll never forget how much those people's presence made on me even to this day.

After following the casket to our seats in the front of the church, I have no memories of the service. I must have blocked it from my mind.

I crawled into the backseat of a big black limo with my sisters after the funeral to make the 15-mile drive to the Catholic cemetery in Farmer City where Sheryl was to be buried. We were all sobbing. Lisa stopped crying long enough to declare that she was going to take care of Sheryl's boys. She said she would help raise them because Sheryl would have done that for her. That was such a huge commitment.

I didn't know how to match that so I said, "OK, we all have to agree right now that no matter what, from this moment on, we all have to agree to cooperate and get along or we'll never be able to take care of Sheryl's boys." We all agreed right then before we got out of the limo at the cemetery that no matter how mad we might get with each other, we would not fight, we would always love each other and ultimately get over it and get along.

I got out of the limo overwhelmed by the vow we had all just taken. The next thing I remember is the casket being lowered into the ground and dirt being thrown on it. It was almost suffocating. We laid bouquets of yellow flowers on the grave while each walking away with a single yellow rose. Sheryl's favorite color was yellow. Mine still sits in a crystal bowl in my china cabinet. I can't bear the thought of ever throwing it away.

In order to jolt myself back to reality and find a way to function, I had to turn to business. I knew I was eventually going to have to return to Florida where John and I lived and had jobs and wouldn't be able to contribute much to physically taking care of them, so I vowed to myself that I would take care of all legal matters. I would make sure Greg was arrested, tried, and convicted, and that "we" had custody of the children and were the ones who would raise them. It was my duty to make sure Greg paid for what he did and that neither he nor his family ever had anything to do with raising Sheryl's children.

John left the day after the funeral and went back to work. I wasn't nearly ready to leave and I certainly couldn't think about going back to work. I had way too much to do right there. I hadn't been at my job very long and only had a week of vacation time. After a week passed, I worked up the nerve to call my boss ready to plead my case for just a little more time. Without even asking, he told me to take another week off. They could handle things at the firm until I returned. Those words were another act of kindness that I'll never forget.

My sisters and their husbands returned to their homes to sleep after the funeral. I stayed with my mom and dad. I began to make plans with Art about what we could do to make sure we could keep the children.

My mother was in a horrible place mentally. She couldn't function. I was angry at her for this. While I thought I understood her trauma, I wanted her to suck it up and, for just a moment, be my mom and comfort me in my sorrow too. She couldn't do it. She never did. After I had my first child, I forgave my mother for this, having a new understanding of the pain it must have caused to have a child murdered.

The boys, 6, 3 and 15 months were deeply traumatized by their last several tumultuous months and their mother's sudden death. The oldest boy often appeared semi-comatose. He was never the same after he found his mother that morning hanging in the garage. When the first emergency responders arrived, he was standing at the door holding the baby, with the middle boy by his side.

FIVE

I talked to Art's associate, Bob Kirchner, every day while I was staying at my mom's as he became the point person when it came to the custody case. I suspected Bob took over in large part because Art couldn't bear the thought of us losing custody of the boys after we lost Sheryl. But it may have simply because of the type of person and lawyer Bob was.

He was a good man, with a kind soul who really cared about his clients. He had a reputation of taking on tough cases and never giving up on winning if he thought his client was in the right.

The judge granted a shelter care order, which gave my mother and father temporary guardianship of the boys the day Sheryl was found dead. This was an enormous relief and gave us a little time to figure things out.

I contacted the women's shelter where Sheryl went for help and they invited us in as a family to talk to them. I was receptive to a group session but even more I wanted to talk to someone who Sheryl had confided in recently for help and who had supported her. My parents didn't understand why we should go but they knew it was important to me so they agreed to it. When we arrived, counselors began to talk to us about abused women and how it's not their fault when things of this nature happen to them.

That was helpful to me as I was starting to have inklings of anger towards Sheryl. How could she have let this happen? Why did she marry the idiot and why didn't she just leave the son-of-a-bitch long ago? It was a different time and people didn't look at abuse the same way as they do now, especially not in rural Illinois. I certainly didn't.

All in all, it was comforting and they strongly recommended that even if we all didn't want counseling, the boys certainly needed it. My parents agreed and sought a counselor for them.

It was impossible to know what to say to them about Sheryl's death. The kids were told that mommy died, she went to heaven and wouldn't be coming back. Considering the oldest was six, in hindsight it was odd to me that he never asked any questions about what really happened. I honestly think he knew how bad things were and was exposed to Greg hurting Sheryl. He didn't ask about the details of the situation because he was afraid of Greg. I told him we were crying because we were sad but that it was all going to be okay and not to worry.

The second week after the murder, we needed to get in the house because the kids didn't have any of their clothes or toys. We got permission from the State's Attorney and the boys' guardian ad litem. Lisa and I drove to the house together, our hearts in our throats.

The first thing I noticed was the yellow crime scene tape around the outside of the house. I got out of the car and approached the garage as if a bogyman man was going to jump out at me at any moment.

I didn't want to see the rope and the ladder next to where she died, but I forced myself not only to look, but to take it all in. I needed to observe everything I could. The investigators had surely missed the clear evidence that she had been murdered and I was bound and determined to find it and report it to the police so they could arrest Greg. Lisa didn't even pause in the garage and walked right in the house.

I scanned the garage as if I were videotaping it with my eyes. I couldn't believe the mess I saw. There was stuff everywhere—full boxes, empty boxes, and piles of clothes and papers. It was like a hurricane had hit. It made sense though. She told me that at the hearing when the judge granted her full custody of the children and possession of the home, he also told her to pack Greg's things. She was being compliant and packing his things.

I saw Greg's fireman's badge laying on the pool table, next to her open purse and a half-eaten candy bar. She had always snacked at night; after she had children, she usually got her candy fix after she put the boys in bed.

Her purse was on the corner of the pool table. We were supposed to be getting clothes and toys for the boys so I didn't go through it as thoroughly as I really wanted to. The first thing I saw in her purse was my business card. This was before cell phones back in the day when we had to write down people's phone numbers. My card had my office number printed on the front and my home number written on the back in Sheryl's writing. One corner of the card was missing and had clearly been chewed off by the youngest boy. I never told Lisa but I took that card that day and placed it in Sheryl's hand the day of her funeral before they closed the casket for the last time. Sheryl talks to me vividly in my dreams and I like to think her having my card is what allows me to continue to have these amazing exchanges with her.

The purse contained her wallet, driver's license, and credit cards which assured me it wasn't a random stranger that killed her. Not that I ever imagined that to be the case but I was determined to gather every fact I could to counter whatever absurd theory Greg proposed. I continued through the pool room and down the stairs to the basement. The washer lid was up, it was full of clothes, and the powdered soap had already been added. All she would have had to do was close the lid and the load would have started. Why didn't she? The clock on the VCR in the basement was flashing.

I wondered if he flipped a fuse and shut her electricity off which is why she left the lid up, went to the door, and laid her candy bar on the pool table.

I went back up the stairs into the kitchen. She had cleaned the house from the front to the back. The kitchen was the last room before the pool room. The vacuum was sitting in the middle of the kitchen floor like she had just moved it to that room. The rest of the house was clean and organized. I tiptoed into the house and began studying the inside. I didn't know what exactly had happened and was desperate to figure it out. I wanted to know every detail. It was as if I thought Sheryl might tell me exactly what befell her if I walked slowly enough through the house.

Lisa and I walked into the dining room at the same time. There on the table was a magazine called *New Woman*. Our eyes met. She would never have had a magazine in the house in the past because Greg never would have let her spend money on such a frivolous item and he would have harassed her to the bitter end over a magazine with such a title. We both looked at each other and cried.

I knew the police found a used condom on the floor in the pool room behind the door leading to the garage. While the pool room was a disaster and she wasn't always known as the best housekeeper, I knew my sister well enough to know she didn't just discard a used condom on the floor in a doorway they used every day. She was a nurse and the mother of three young boys; there was no reason that condom was there other than that Greg had raped her before, or perhaps after, he killed her.

Lisa continued to gather the boys' belongings while I ventured into the bedroom. The bed was unmade. At the foot of the bed were the clothes she wore that day. She must have stepped out of them to put on her nightgown and left them lie in a heap like she had done when we were growing up. She was getting ready to go to bed. I cried again. She had no idea when she got ready for bed that night that she wasn't going to get up in the morning.

Her radio alarm clock was flashing like the VCR clock in the basement. The telephone on the nightstand had an unused Kleenex laying on top of the telephone receiver and an empty pill bottle was on the dresser with the lid off. With the way the investigation went, I still think that that bottle on the dresser had some significance to her death.

The Kleenex confused me too. Sheryl had allergies and her nose ran all the time so Kleenex around Sheryl weren't unusual. What was unusual is the way it was laid across the phone receiver totally unused and barely handled. Why would that be placed there just so?

The aggravated criminal sexual assault was still pending, he had been indicted but the case was still in the early stages. Greg and his attorney were well aware of the consequences of the charges. Hayes wrote Art a letter on September 21, 1990, which said, "You may wish to amend your pleading. Your client has procured much more serious charges than those alleged in your pleading. Your client has procured information charging my client with One Count of Aggravated Criminal Sexual Assault, a class X felony; Two Counts of Criminal Sexual Assault, a Class I Felony; and One Count of unlawful restraint. If convicted as charged, my client will be sentenced to the penitentiary-no probation or other sentence being available to the judge. I call this matter to your attention so that you may be aware that the costs of defense will be a substantial charge against the marital estate."

He killed her for two reasons. He would never let her get away, that would mean she had won, and he could never allow that. More importantly, he had to keep her from testifying or he would most likely go to prison.

Greg was not going to let that happen even if it meant he had to kill her. Greg was never wrong and he always won. He didn't want to be exposed as the monster he was.

His family, the guys at Jim's Tap, at work, and the fire department couldn't know who he really was. Sheryl was a lying psycho bitch who, according to him, had postpartum depression, abused the children, used drugs, spent money uncontrollably, and was having an affair. He had mastered the art of gaslighting.

I talked to Roger Simpson, the county State's Attorney shortly after her death. He was from the suburbs of Chicago, had relocated to Monticello, and was elected to the State's Attorney for Piatt County in October of 1988. Roger was a young, good looking, and charming man who had a way with words. I felt we were in good hands.

I hadn't spoken to him about the sexual assault case as there had not been a reason for me to do so. However, now that Sheryl was dead, I had a lot of questions about the investigation and why Greg had not been arrested. I wanted to make sure he fully intended to take the aggravated criminal sexual assault to trial no matter what. He committed to taking it to trial. He may have done that in part to appease me in some respect. The investigation had not produced evidence in his mind that was sufficient to make an arrest. He had to give me something to get me off his back for a bit. I couldn't understand what he was waiting on to make the arrest. He looked me in the eyes shortly after her death and told me he knew Greg killed my sister but he needed evidence to tie Greg to the scene of the crime.

This didn't comfort me. I said, "For one thing, we know he killed her and for another, what are you going to do about the sexual assault? From the very beginning I knew he killed her, family and friends knew he killed her, the state's attorney knew, even the judge knew he killed her. It seemed like everyone did, but yet he still walked free."

I was not going to let him even hint at dropping those charges. I was a young woman, but I had enough perseverance, determination, and perhaps, naivety to put the pressure on, keep it on, and hold his feet to the fire.

Roger had a way of saying just the right things to me to ease the pressure on himself. "You know there is no statute of limitations on murder, Renee. Just let it all play out. Someone will slip up. Someone will talk and we'll have him." He agreed to go along with the sexual assault trial to get testimony that could be used later even if Greg walked.

Upon seeing Sheryl hanging in the garage, the local sheriff's department immediately called in the Illinois State Police. Things were different back then regarding domestic abuse and police protocols and the local sheriffs didn't have much experience with homicide cases in Piatt County, Illinois.

Roger was at the scene of the crime. He told me later he knew it was a murder and was stunned to hear a local police officer on the scene say he thought it was suicide. Greg's family and johnny-on-the-spot attorney, Keith Hayes, also came to the scene and immediately started their spin campaign. They felt so bad that Sheryl was so distraught from postpartum depression that she would take her own life.

The story leading up to her death left those who were familiar with it certain of her murder. However, those who didn't know the back story saw what appeared to be a suicide, although one that was questionable.

I continued to investigate the case myself because I began to think no one else was going to do anything. I called Roger all the time and talked about my theories. There were so many things that pointed to Greg's guilt.

There was no forced entry. This made no sense at all. She was afraid of him, she would have locked the doors for certain. Either he got in without forced entry because he had a key or she let him in, which is a possibility.

She had a pattern of some sort imprinted on her back. It looked like it may have come from one of the rubber mats that were placed in the bottom of a bathtub to keep you from slipping. She had dirt on the backs of her heels and a rug burn on at least one elbow. Perhaps she died flat on her back and was dragged across the dirty garage floor which would have put the dirt on her heels.

When Brandon found her, she was in a sitting position. She was hanging but her butt was only about 6 inches off the ground and her feet were in front of her with the ladder placed next to her. It was impossible that she had hung herself; she could have just stood up. The scene was supposed to look like she jumped off the ladder but it made no sense. She couldn't have hung herself unless the rope slipped.

We eventually got rope experts involved because, if it hadn't slipped, the rope would be frayed. The ligature marks around her neck were horizontal and if you die from hanging from a rope, they go up and back at an angle because of the weight, not vertical.

Were things so bad that she committed suicide? That simply was not possible.

She had just ordered kids Halloween costumes, planned a party, had a bed on layaway, she was talking to me often and was almost joyful, why would she kill herself now?

Only one thing made sense. Greg murdered my sister. But still, he walked free.

SIX

And where did Greg say he was when my sister died?

On the night of October 4, 1990, Bob Henderson threw a going away party for T-Byrd because he was leaving town for Wisconsin to work on his brother's dairy farm. The timing of all of this was peculiar. He told his employer he was quitting his job to leave for Wisconsin on the 3rd, the party was on the 4th, and my sister was found dead on the 5th. Why was he in such a hurry to get out of town?

Sheryl didn't attend the party, but she did drop by T-Byrd's house after she left work. When she arrived, he was packing his truck and they talked for a bit. Then she went to our parents' house to pick up the kids and went home. Chris and Jackie drove by Sheryl's house and saw her unloading boxes from her Blazer. Later, it turned out these were documents she had been storing at my parents' house for safe keeping. She finally felt safe enough to bring them home. They were on the pool table when her body was found.

T-Byrd stayed at his going away party until midnight. Greg showed up, but left around 8, which is kind of odd considering T-Byrd was one of his best friends. Greg planned to spend the night at his grandparents' house, which was also more than a bit strange considering he hadn't stayed with them since he was a kid.

He showed up at his grandparents' house a bit after 8 p.m. He said he didn't bring a change of clothes. His father,

John Houser, contradicted Greg, saying he took a change of clothes with him to go to his grandparents' house.

Around 10:30 that night, Jackie saw a bathroom light as well as the garage door lights on at Sheryl's house.

Les was the last to leave the party at 1 a.m. A local police officer, Deputy Dunlap, saw Les driving around at 1:40 a.m. near Greg's grandparents' house. He verified the license plates just to make sure it was him. Les was alone. After going around the block, Dunlap saw Les in the truck again, except this time he had someone in his truck with him. Dunlap could not identify the passenger but who else would it have been other than Greg?

The morning of October 5, Sheryl was found dead in the garage. Her time of death was estimated to be between 1 and 4 a.m.

Greg got up around 6 a.m. and left his grandparents' house to go back to his parents' house and take a shower. He returned to his grandparents' house around 7 a,m. ate breakfast, and then he and his grandpa went to the fire station to wash his truck. He was there when the call came in about Sheryl's death.

To anyone who knew Greg, none of his activities the evening before made any sense. He would never have left a party early, stayed with his grandparents, ate breakfast with his grandparents, showered at home, and then taken his grandpa to the fire station early on a Friday morning to wash his truck. Especially because it was the week of Greg's vacation, a week he always went hunting every year prior. It was obvious to so many of us that he was cleverly, or so he thought, setting up his alibi.

In Illinois, a cause of death is listed on the death certificate. Normally, the local coroner fills out the form with notations such as "natural" and then a secondary reason, such as "heart attack" or "cancer". If the cause of death was not apparent, the law allows the coroner to convene a coroner's jury, present evidence, and ask the jury to determine the cause of death. The jury has to select one of four outcomes: natural, undetermined, homicide, or suicide. Once the primary cause is determined by the jury, the coroner filled out the details on the death certificate. While the coroner's jury has no legal significance on a criminal or civil case, it was important to me and my family that Sheryl's cause of death be listed as a homicide. After all, we all knew that Greg killed Sheryl.

At the very least, I was adamant that Sheryl's cause of death was not listed as a suicide. There was no evidence of that and to list it as such would have been sheer laziness on the part of law enforcement and the other professionals, in my opinion. It wasn't true and a suicide on her death certificate had ramifications to my family. Sheryl was Catholic and it would have been extremely hard on my mother to have the cause of death be listed as suicide. Further, the life insurance policy Greg took out on her just months before her murder most likely would not have been paid. That money, while the least of my family's concerns, is what put Sheryl's three boys through college.

I talked to Roger before I left home to return to Florida. I wanted his commitment that he would not drop the aggravated attempted sexual assault case and that he still planned to take that case to trial. He gave me his word and assured me that he would pursue that case no matter what because he believed it could have positive impacts on the murder investigation. He felt that someone else other than Greg was involved in Sheryl's murder or at least knew Greg did it and would eventually talk. The assault trial gave him the opportunity to obtain testimony from Greg and his buddies. Roger had not previously tried a murder case but I had hopes that he would be vying for a big win early in his career so he would work hard and fight relentlessly for a murder conviction.

He told me the first order of business was to complete her death certificate which required a cause of death. He explained the coroner's jury process to me and assured me that his primary objective was to allow as little of the evidence as possible to be presented. His strategy was to keep the details of her death out of the media and not let Greg and his buddies know what we knew. He wanted to keep them in fear again in hopes that the stress would get to one of them and they would talk.

Roger assured me that the inquest had no legal significance and his strategy to reveal very little information made it an event that I didn't need to make the trip back home for. I really wanted to be present, but when Art provided additional assurance of the unimportance of the inquest and that he would attend on the family's behalf, I saved my precious time off and money and did not return for the inquest which was held on January 23, 1991.

My dad, Lisa, Julie, Renee Monfort, and various other friends and supporters were in attendance. I was so uptight about missing the proceeding that my sister Julie tape recorded the whole thing for me to listen to later.

When I talked to Julie and Lisa after the inquest, they told me the jury ruled Sheryl's cause of death as "undetermined". It felt like someone hit me in the stomach. Lisa told me that it really seemed like Roger, the investigators, and the coroner carefully controlled the evidence (which I knew was the plan all along) and led the jury to the conclusion of, "Undetermined." Perhaps it was that part I had not mentally prepared for.

In my mind, there was only one option. It was homicide. But with how things had gone with Greg not having been arrested and walking free, talking about how sad it was that his loving wife was so distraught that she committed suicide, I had prepared myself for that outcome. But "undetermined" really caught me off guard.

I had not prepared my mom for that outcome. I tried to explain to her Roger's strategy and how we should be grateful that the jury didn't come back with a verdict of suicide, but she couldn't understand or maybe just refused to accept anything other than what we all knew happened to Sheryl. She had been murdered by her abusive, controlling husband in the middle of a divorce to save his reputation and ego and to keep him out of prison. While I still wanted to trust Roger and be assured that he would ultimately obtain justice for Sheryl, my first doubts had crept in.

While we were committed to seeing justice done, which meant Greg being arrested for murder, our more immediate concern were custody issues. It was bad enough that he murdered Sheryl but we couldn't let a monster who choked the life out of a human and strung them up from a rafter in their garage like a dead deer raise these children. At best, he would raise them to be like him and at worst, he might kill one or all of them. Neither of those outcomes were an option for us.

We knew that Greg never wanted custody of the boys. He didn't want them or take care of them when Sheryl was alive. He certainly didn't want to be burdened with them now. However, he was angry that we were still causing problems for him, so he turned his anger on me, my sisters, and my parents. There was nothing he would do to continue to cause us pain if we weren't willing to let him off the hook for murdering Shery—which, of course, we weren't willing to do.

While all of our desires were to pursue Greg for her murder and custody of the boys, there was a certain reality we had to face. The farming industry had struggled since the late 80s and hadn't yet turned around. My parents were struggling financially. While my parents had agreed to pay for our college educations, I had to assume my undergraduate loan from them when I graduated law school and add that onto the $40,000 debt I graduated from law school with, despite working as a Law Clerk for a local attorney all through law school and limiting my spending and food budget to $30 per week. I was so broke I ate popcorn for dinner because it provided a sense of being full.

The financial situation of my parents and myself compounded my stress. My dad could barely make ends meet before and now he was trying to fight for custody, fund a private investigation of his daughter's murder, and raise three young children. I had no idea where the money was going to come from.

That first Christmas after her death, my parents gave us some money as a gift. Julie and I conferred and both sent that money to Art and Bob to be applied to their attorney's fees and costs without having ever said a word to them. We didn't talk to Lisa about it because she was in a different financial situation than Julie and I and we never wanted to make her feel bad. Over time, I continued to send extra money in whenever I could with the largest single payment being $600.00.

Finally, I decided that I had to talk to Bob about money. My parents weren't going to be able to afford the standard hourly rates but yet we couldn't give up. Bob had a heart of gold and wasn't going to let Greg get custody if he could help it. When I talked to him about my parent's financial situation, he listened empathetically and told me he would talk to Art and see if they could work out some kind of arrangement. Bob got back to me and said that after he discussed the situation with Art, Art agreed that the firm would agree to represent my parents in the custody case at the reduced hourly rate of $100.00 per hour or the flat fee of $8,000. I was just starting out as an attorney and my hourly rate on such matters was $125.00 per hour so I knew the offer was a bargain. I also had some exposure to cases costing $5,000 to $10,000 to take all the way through trial so I thought the $8,000 was probably a good deal. Little did I know then that litigation over custody would last for more than a decade.

I called my dad when I got a copy of the letter and outlined the two fee options. He and I both agreed that the

$8,000 flat fee was probably the slightly better deal so we agreed that that was the option he would choose.

I never asked my dad if he had that money or where that money was going to come from because I knew it didn't matter. I knew he would do whatever it took to make that payment. I felt terrible about the financial burden placed on him and knew that I had to step up my personal contribution to the case. I talked to my friend Renee who agreed that she and I would both work with Bob and help him with legal matters. Renee was practicing in Champaign where Art and Bob were located. She knew them both and agreed to do whatever legal research she could to help Bob out with the custody case. I focused on guiding my parents through the legal quagmire, while at the same time trying to keep my mom sane enough so no one would question her fitness to raise the boys and keep the criminal cases on track.

Sometime between 5 and 6, at the end of my workday, I spun my chair around to my credenza where I kept all my files on Sheryl's case. The first thing I did was call Bob to catch up with him at the end of his day. I was usually the last thing that stood between him and his leaving the office to go home at night. I never met his wife, but I felt like I knew her from our conversations. I felt bad for her because he spent so much time and energy on our case and became not only our legal advocate but my personal friend and confidant. I rarely talked to John about the case and he never asked about it or how I was handling the entire situation. On the other hand, Bob knew my efforts and listened with an open ear whenever I needed to vent, have a breakdown, or just needed a little mental encouragement to keep going.

In hindsight, I'm saddened by the fact that Bob passed away before I realized and truly appreciated how much he cared and did for me and my family. I can only imagine the impact this case had on his personal life. Thus, to Gerri his wife, I wish to thank you from the bottom of my heart for so selfishly allowing your husband to do everything he did for me and my family. Thanks to you both, the boys were raised by my parents and not by Greg's monstruous family, all graduated from college, have wives, gainful employment, and Sheryl's grandchildren.

I owe Renee immensely too. Thanks to her unrelentless research we found a custody case that gave us a leg to stand on. She was also invaluable to me on as a sounding board for the criminal case and of course, as a friend and primary supporter of me, my family, and our efforts.

So many questions remained, ones that no one really seemed to be paying attention to. Why would Sheryl kill herself when everything was finally going so well, and why would she do so right in the middle of doing laundry? None of it made any sense.

And even odder, the used condom found in the pool room, right at a door that led to the garage. For whatever reason, no one thought it was significant, like it was possible she was having sex with random people and that was where it wound up. Sheryl was a very conservative person, there is no way she would have just been having sex with just anyone. And even if she was, would she just leave a condom on the floor and not pick it up? Never. She had three little boys and the condom was found at the back door they used as their primary entry and exit from the house.

Greg refused to use a condom or in any way be responsible for birth control which is why Sheryl used a diaphragm. He had advised her on numerous occasions that he wasn't using a condom and birth control was her problem to deal with.

Whoever killed Sheryl raped her and didn't want there to be any DNA evidence. Who else would have done that but Greg? It was just another part of his planned set up. He wasn't going to leave any evidence which would connect him to the scene.

We investigated any angle we could think of. Roger consulted with experts in multiple areas. He wrote a medical examiner in Chicago to find out about suicides by hanging where there were three loops in the rope. He consulted with a couple different investigators, one of whom was Rod Englert, now known as one of the top forensics consultants in the world.

Roger consulted the FBI on whether they had a rope expert, which they no longer did. So, we looked for a private one. Even Grant Johnson, the local medical examiner, wrote to another medical examiner inquiring about whether he thought it was a suicide versus a homicide based on the number of loops around her neck and the unique knot that was used.

In the meantime, my parents struggled with taking care of three little boys, all of whom had suffered trauma. Lisa had a daughter named Allison who was their age and she brought her over to my mom's and helped take care of the boys every day. Allison grew up thinking she had three older brothers.

My mother's mental health was not good at this time as she was overwhelmed with grief. It was hard for her to take care of three young grandchildren. All of us were very worried about her.

The Aggravated Sexual Assault case against Greg was still pending. While Greg had gotten away with murder, at least up to this point in time, he could still be sent to prison. The sentencing allowed for him to be sentenced to up to 6 years, but realistically, with no prior record, if convicted, he might serve 1 to 2 years. That would certainly be better than nothing. Some punishment for his horrific actions would have been better than none at all. A conviction would give us the chance to get the boys and hopefully by the time he was released there would be a break in the murder case and he would be charged for that.

Roger knew Greg killed Sheryl because he didn't want to go to prison because of the sexual assault. But the problem was that Greg's plan so far had worked. Without her to testify against him, he had a chance at getting away with it. Roger had previously told Sheryl when she was alive that it was a hard case to prove without an eyewitness. According to him, it was just a "he said, she said case." Still, there was no doubt Roger worked hard at preparing the case for trial.

Roger continued to think someone would talk. He still felt that Tim Byrd and Les Shores knew something. In his opinion, Shores had no problem keeping it inside of him but Byrd did.

Tim Byrd is still a bit of a mystery to me. I have no doubt Les Shores was a part of it, but Tim was a friend to Sheryl.

I talked to Tim when I called him on October 12, 1990. Sheryl stopped by his house in Mansfield at 6, because she wanted to say goodbye, but she didn't go to his going away party for obvious reasons. She got to Mom's at 6:40 meaning she hung out at Tim's house for a bit. Would he really have just spent time with her when she came by to say goodbye knowing she would be murdered?

He told me that when she arrived he was loading his truck to move to the dairy farm. He said she was there around 20 minutes. I asked what she was wearing and he said a blue tee-shirt. He said he respected her and didn't take sides when it came to her relationship with Greg. I asked if she was depressed. He said, "No, she was just Sheryl."

I asked if she had a friend she confided in.

He said, "Yes. Me."

I've wondered many times if Tim really thinks that Sheryl was his friend. If she was, he certainly let her down in a very big way; one that turned out to be fatal.

There was quite a bit of pretrial publicity in our community. It didn't focus on the sexual assault case; it was more around her death. Roger told me he was comfortable that the state would prevail but it would be difficult as the jury would have to vote to convict without Sheryl as a witness. To complicate matters, when she initially went to the emergency room, she didn't tell hospital staff about the sexual assault. She went back the next day and told them what Greg had done. They did a rape kit at that time but it was too late to collect any evidence.

Greg continued to be represented by his attorney, Keith Hayes. Nothing had changed when it came to Hayes. He still had no ethics at all, there was nothing he wouldn't do, which is exactly what made him dangerous. After Sheryl's murder, when I started working with Roger, he told me, "Hayes can't be trusted." It was a small county, and Hayes had a reputation that Roger knew all too well.

Hayes knew the sexual assault case could be damaging when it came to Greg being prosecuted for murder. Court testimony could go poorly for Greg and anything said on the stand could be used in a potential murder case down the road. Hayes filed a motion for change of venue saying it wouldn't be possible for Greg to get a fair case in Piatt County. His stated reasons were the adverse publicity surrounding the murder as well as that the judge was the same judge in the divorce case who had recently held a Shelter Care hearing and placed the physical custody of the boys with my parents.

Hayes won the motion for change of venue and the case was moved to Macon County which was bigger than Piatt County. It was primarily a blue-collar county known for having a large grain elevator and a high crime rate. Decatur, which was the county seat, had a different newspaper and news station than we did locally, so the case had not had nearly the publicity there as in Piatt County. This was all before the internet when what happened the next county over in rural Illinois sometimes remained pretty much unknown.

By November, Art, Bob, and I were concerned about what would happen if the judge dismissed the divorce case. The boys could revert to Greg's custody which was our worst fear. We were fairly certain that my parents, as grandparents, did not have standing or the right to seek custody of their grandchild with one parent alive without proving Greg was unfit. At the beginning of November, Art and Bob filed a juvenile petition for custody alleging Greg abused the children, and assaulted Sheryl, seeking a Shelter Care Hearing and order adjudging that the boys should be wards of the court. Our strategy was to make sure my parents had a case pending if the judge were to dismiss the divorce case because of Sheryl's death. According to the statute, a juvenile case had to be heard within 180 days of filing.

DCFS decided the boys had to visit their father every other weekend. When the dreaded time came, a social worker arrived at the house to pick up the boys to take them to visit Greg. Often, he would have to get out of the car and pry Brandon's fingers off of my mom and shove him in the car and force the door shut before he could get out. Throughout all of this, Brandon would scream at the top of his lungs. One time, he jumped out the window of the car before it could drive away.

When they returned, it would take hours for my mom and Lisa to calm the boys back down. They came home like wild animals running, jumping, screaming, and crying and being aggressive to each other.

The trial was scheduled for January when Sheryl was alive. However, after her murder, the case was continued a few times because of various pretrial motions. Finally, the trial began. We were all optimistic about the result. At least if he were sent to prison for sexually assaulting Sheryl, he wouldn't be totally getting away with things and he wouldn't be getting custody of the boys.

We were going to trial.

SEVEN

In May of 1991, I returned to Illinois to attend Greg's sexual assault trial with my family. As I sat in the pews of the small courtroom and listened to the testimony, all sorts of feelings washed over me. My sister was dead, Greg had killed her after assaulting her multiple times, yet I was sitting there listening to him say none of it ever happened, only to be followed by Les who testified that he was there the night of the alleged sexual assault and he didn't hear a thing.

It was all so raw. I couldn't contain my emotions. I had thrown myself into investigating the case so thoroughly that I never really processed what I was feeling. Looking back, maybe some of that was on purpose. I immediately escaped back to Florida, lived my life far away like nothing ever happened, and added Sheryl's case to my caseload as if my family was just another client.

I wasn't prepared for seeing Greg in person. I hadn't seen him since before he had killed Sheryl. When I first laid eyes on him, I almost had a panic attack. I started hyperventilating. I couldn't breathe. I began to understand why people lost control in courtrooms and attacked defendants. I wanted to stand up and go after him, but thankfully I restrained myself.

He was so arrogant and pompous when he took the stand. If I had any doubt about it before, I realized then that he truly is a sociopath. He had no sign of nervousness at all. It was like he knew he was going to beat the charge and walk free. His family was there, of course. It made my blood boil to see them pretend to act like they were so sad that Sheryl committed suicide.

At one point, there was a break in the trial and Greg left the courtroom. Throughout the trial, he was always led out through a side door and down a hall. I quickly exited to the back of the courtroom on a mission to find him. I wasn't even sure what I was going to do if and when I did, but I knew I wanted to lay my eyes on him without anyone else around. I went down the hall and looked in each room until I found him in a library where he was sitting alone at a table near the door. He had no place to hide.

I thought to myself, "Oh, there you are, you son of a bitch."

I stepped quietly into the room. When he looked up and saw me standing there, he had a look on his face that said, "Oh shit."

He began to scan the room for someone to tell me to get out of there, but there was no one around; it was just me and him. He looked down at the table, pursed his lips, and proceeded to ignore me. Or at least he tried to. I wasn't going to let that happen.

I took another step or two into the room and said, "You son of a bitch, I know you killed my sister. Look at me, look me in the eyes, and tell me you didn't kill my sister."

He didn't respond. He just put his head down and pursed his lips even tighter and continued to ignore me. I took a few more steps forward and bent my head down close to his face and said, "Look at me, look me in the eyes and tell me you didn't kill her."

He wouldn't do it. A few minutes later, someone came into the room. I can't remember who. And I was told to leave.

If I had even the smallest doubt that he killed her, I didn't anymore. I knew even more from then on. All he had to do was look at me and say he was innocent and he couldn't do it. He was such a coward.

Hayes had the gall to try and move for a mistrial because of my actions but the judge denied it. I was told to behave myself, to stay away from Greg from now on, and not to talk to the media. I didn't regret what I did but I was embarrassed that his attorney made an issue out of the encounter and that my actions could have caused a mistrial. I told myself that I would have to control myself from then on. He was going to pay for what he did to Sheryl and if he didn't pay, it couldn't be because of something I did to jeopardize the case.

We didn't have a chance from the start at getting a conviction. At the trial, the victim normally sat at the prosecution table even if she didn't testify, but of course this didn't happen because Sheryl was dead. We would have to rely on her testimony from the motion for custody after the assault. Without a live witness, Art, Bob, and others told me it was an uphill battle. I must have chosen not to hear them because all I can remember is Roger telling me how confident he was that he could win. However, my notes are clear—plenty of other attorneys told me the odds were slim. Hayes made a pretrial motion asking the judge to not let Roger tell the jury that Sheryl was not at the trial because she was dead. The judge ruled that a statement could be read to the jury that she was not there because she was deceased but nothing else could be said about the suspicious nature of her death.

In my mind, that is the primary reason we lost. Back then, and even now, a lot of people think it is a victim that presses charges and not the district attorney, so her being deceased had to influence the jurors' decisions. Many of them must have thought Sheryl didn't even care what happened. If she did, why didn't she attend the trial and testify? We were not able to bring up the other numerous incidences of abuse. That was the law back then. So, the jury had no idea of the history of the case or the fact that Greg was being investigated for her murder.

When Greg was acquitted, it was like being punched in the gut all over again. Even if he got away with murdering Sheryl, at least if he was convicted, he would be in prison and punished for something. At my weakest moments, I even wondered if maybe he drove her to suicide...just maybe. But I knew for a fact he sexually assaulted her. At least he had to pay for that.

But he didn't.

I was devastated.

Greg got away with sexually assaulting my sister and it looked like he was going to get away with her murder too. To make matters worse, we needed this win for the custody case. If he had been convicted and gone to prison, we could have overcome my parents' lack of standing issue and all the other issues in the custody case.

Adding salt to my wounds was seeing the look on Greg's face when the verdict of not guilty was read. It started as the familiar smirk I knew all too well followed by a full-blown smile. He walked out of the courtroom with a bounce in his step. He got away with it, and he was never going to get caught. He was home free and he could hurt us even more by now getting custody of the boys.

I locked eyes with Roger as he turned and watched Greg leave the courtroom a free man. I knew from the look in his eyes he had suffered an enormous blow. I wondered then if he would ever be able to bring himself to charge Greg with Sheryl's murder. In a way, I didn't blame him. I had grown close to Roger over the last several months. He knew what happened to Sheryl and I know he genuinely wanted Greg to pay.

It was hard to get over Greg going free. I was crushed and my parents even more so. I went back to Florida, like a wounded dog with its tail between its legs, to my husband and my job. At least I didn't wake up seeing my family every day, so I was able to lose myself in my work. The guilt I felt knowing my family was left in Illinois to provide the care and comfort to three traumatized boys whose fate was uncertain was almost unbearable. I had to compensate and the only way I knew to do that was to work harder on the murder investigation and the custody case.

I was concerned now that Greg was found not guilty that his fight against us for custody would intensify. In his mind, the verdict proved to everyone he didn't abuse Sheryl. Now all he had to do was get custody of the boys and show everyone once and for all that Sheryl was so distraught she committed suicide. This would put him on a pedestal in his parents' eyes and hurt my parents. He didn't care about the boys back then and he still doesn't. It was just all about winning.

John continued to live in Fort Lauderdale during the week. I had no one to come home to, so often I didn't. I worked until 8 or 9, drove home, ate quickly, and fell asleep on the couch night after night.

My life became reminiscent of the weeks before the murder. My mother continued to call me constantly asking me what I was doing to change what happened. Not only did she want me to investigate the murder, have him arrested and convicted, she needed me to make sure that she and my dad obtained custody of the boys. Perhaps even more taxing to me, she needed to express her emotions—all of them, whether they be anger, sadness, and depression. I had no one to turn to in order to express my own feelings or obtain some emotional support. John was not physically present often and when he was, all we talked it was about him and his career.

We weren't done, though. We hadn't even started to fight. By the end of March, Roger continued to seek out expert opinions from well-known homicide investigators, rope experts, DNA experts, and medical examiners.

While all this was going on, we temporarily lost custody of Brandon. Greg's motion to dismiss the divorce case finally went to hearing and the judge dismissed the case, writing, "the Order of Guardianship of the minor children by the Department of Children and Family Services in the minor children is revoked and custody is transferred to Greg."

Thankfully, on September 11, 1991, the court reconsidered its decision and DCFS retained custody of the kids. Mom and Dad picked Brandon up at Greg's parents' house. He was extremely upset and my mother had to explain to Brandon that she didn't know this was going to happen.

Life went on and things settled into a routine, albeit one that was not very pleasant. Lisa did household chores to help my mom and dad, and my mom kept calling me every day asking for my help. She was a mess, and rightfully so. She wasn't functioning well and she couldn't let it go. She couldn't accept it. She just kept telling me I had to do something; I had to fix it.

While I don't want her to feel bad about it now, she put me in an extremely difficult position. There I was, 24 years old, and it was my problem to figure out; something I needed to solve. The pressure was enormous. I felt responsible for my mother's mental state, thinking that if I fixed all the legal problems, I could fix her feelings too. I felt an immense amount of guilt because I was in Florida while Lisa helped take care of the kids, so I compensated even more and took on that responsibility.

My life was empty. I didn't do anything but work my day job and work on the case every night and on the weekends.

To make things worse, John, the man I married, continued to show me how selfish he was. I don't have any memories of him during that time. It was like he didn't exist. He was all about himself. He flew airplanes for a living so he was away often. If he wanted to do something and included me, it was fine because he could be fun to hang out with. But he wasn't about supporting me as a person who had gone through a trauma. I don't remember talking to him about any of this or letting him know how much I was working on it. He was just gone.

We didn't have laptops back then, so I stayed at my work every night and used Lexus and Westlaw and researched cases and theories and laws. Everyone else went home, but I stayed, sometimes until 9 or 10 at night. I spent a lot of time talking to Bob because we had an hour's time difference. I could often catch him before he left to go home. If Roger wasn't going to do anything, Bob and I could at least work on custody and the wrongful death suit which might get something going in a criminal case. If nothing else, maybe we could get a civil declaration that he murdered her.

At least that would be something.

EIGHT

Everyone knew Greg killed Sheryl. It was the town's worst-kept secret.

But yet he just kept living his life, doing the same sort of things he always did, some mundane and some terrible.

Greg took pleasure in torturing my parents and not following through when it came to some of the minor things he was supposed to do when it came to the children. Nothing was ever easy. Greg was never allowed to do an exchange of custody. At first, it had to be through DCFS and then, after a while, his parents were allowed to pick up the boys. The exchange would be made in the local IGA parking lot. My father would never even consider letting a Houser on his property.

Other than Greg's scheduled visits, he never saw the boys. Visitation was mostly so his parents could save face and show the town they cared. John and Caroline were never nice to my parents. It was almost like our family was the problem for not being more understanding about Greg murdering Sheryl.

When the kids went to the Houser's, most of the time they wouldn't come back with the items they left home with. My mother would never let the kids go over there with anything nice because my parents couldn't afford to buy new sneakers or hats and mittens and coats every week.

The boys never had much of a relationship with Greg. They had to go visit him, he was their dad after all, but he hadn't changed. He wasn't a nice person to be around.

He always had a girlfriend, from the moment Sheryl died to when he went to jail, he always had someone in his life. It really says a lot that a guy like Greg had no problem finding women to spend time with.

These so-called girlfriends would start out not being nice to my mother because Greg would tell them Sheryl was a crazy lady he was married to who committed suicide and my family kept harassing him. He was the victim, not Sheryl, and the sad part was these women would believe him.

But soon his true colors would come out and he would start to become abusive. Then these women would think to themselves maybe, just maybe, Greg killed Sheryl after all.

Later, some of these women ended up talking to the police and telling them about their relationships with Greg. One of them was Christie Campbell who met Greg at a bar when she was 25. She didn't know about Sheryl at first, but eventually Greg told her about his previous marriage and said Sheryl killed herself because she was depressed. At one point they planned on getting married, but her family was concerned because of Greg's past so they put off the wedding which caused him to pout and get angry. According to Christie, he occasionally would act violent and punch the wall next to her head.

Another girlfriend was Deanna Quinn. Once, during a fight, Greg told her, "You'll hang for that." She replied, "just like you did to Sheryl." After that, Greg stopped talking. He was mentally and physically abusive to her and called her charming names, such as, "gutter slut." He slapped her, pushed her, and threw things at her. Once during a fight, he threw a Molotov cocktail at her front door. According to Deanna, at one point Greg and Les went to Wisconsin and beat up Tim to make him keep his mouth shut.

One woman, Vicki Houser, actually married Greg. She met Greg in late 1996 at a bar in Mansfield, IL. About six weeks later, they got married. She said Greg was "so nice and friendly" before they got married, but after they were married, he changed.

Approximately two weeks before marrying Greg, she found out Sheryl had committed suicide. The day after she married, her mother told her there were rumors either Greg or his brother killed Sheryl.

After getting married, she described Greg as a 1950s husband who expected her to cook and clean and have supper ready for him when he get home from work. Greg was very demanding and had to know where Vicki was at all times and what she was doing. Greg verbally abused her and was demeaning in the way he spoke to her. She described Greg as getting mad easily and yelling at her. A lot of the yelling and screaming came when Vicki had not prepared a meal or done something Greg expected of her. Greg threw things at Vicki when they would fight and he would grab her arm and say he was not done yet when they were fighting. She said he was a "disturbed person."

Greg told her he and Sheryl had been fighting because he had told Sheryl he only wanted two children and when she got pregnant, he wanted nothing to do with the baby, even after it was born. So she went out in the garage and hung herself somehow.

Greg told Vicki they had a trial and they cleared him and he "walked out laughing."

In October of 1997, Vicki began sleeping on the couch because she did not want to deal with Greg anymore. In December of 1997, she and her daughter took off on Greg. They loaded up their clothes and a few things and left everything else behind.

Years later, Greg found out he was legally married to Vicki. He said he didn't think the person who married them actually had the authority to do so. And Vicki found out that she was not divorced. Evidently, she thought she had taken steps to divorce Greg but that was not the case. Vicki was able to serve him with divorce papers and legally divorce him.

It was difficult to know what to tell the boys. There was never any conversation between us and them about Greg killing Sheryl. We don't know if Greg ever said anything to them but I assume not. It was taboo. How could we tell them their father killed their mother when they had to go spend every other weekend with him? This awful thing just remained unspoken, but it was always close to all of us, hanging over our heads. Still though, they had to have known, they had to have heard the rumors.

My mom gritted her teeth and fought through her feelings and kept her thoughts to herself around the boys. But it was hard, we all hated Greg, we never asked the boys how it was when they were with him. Greg spent time hunting with them or he would help them work on their cars when they were older but that was pretty much the extent of their relationship.

I am sure, as time went on, he thought he was home free. Nothing was going to happen to him. He got away with killing my sister, the mother of his children, and apparently it didn't bother him one bit.

His life went on unencumbered although it didn't go particularly well. He continued to work as a diesel mechanic after Sheryl's death but over time he got work doing menial jobs such as driving trucks and changing windshields at a glass replacement store.

He was always a heavy drinker when he was with Sheryl and he continued to be after he killed her. He had a stool at the local bar he sat on from when he got out of work until he stumbled home at night. People might talk to him and say hey, but most gave him a wide berth. Some who did talk to him probably justified it by the fact if he hadn't been arrested, he probably wasn't guilty.

He wasn't popular around town. He remained an ass and a hothead. He still had his loyal friends, Les and T-Byrd, but it might have been they all stayed in contact to make sure no one ever squealed on each other.

Other than spending time at the bar, he became a bit of a recluse. His hair got long, he grew a big, unkempt beard, and became really overweight.

The boys played football and basketball. There would be times when I would be home, I would see him at one of their games and almost start to hyperventilate because I would get so upset. At a basketball game, he would either stand in a doorway and make an appearance or sit way up high in the bleachers, never with anyone or never interacting with anyone. It was almost like everyone thought, "Hey look, here is the killer, who came to watch his kids play basketball."

Of course, if you lost your mother in any way there would be some emotional issues, but it was hard to tell how any of this trauma affected the boys. They were active kids and they grew up on the farm with my dad, living a life somewhat like the way Sheryl grew up. My mother said the middle one was most impacted by Sheryl's death. He often would stand in a chair looking out the window and wait for Sheryl to come home. My mother was really worried about him.

The human brain has a great way of protecting itself, but, at some point, trauma had to still be there for all of them. The oldest boy found her dead body. Sheryl would scream for the boys when Greg attacked her. Did she scream for them that night? Did any of them get up and hear or see Greg? Who is to say Greg didn't threaten them?

Over the years, we talked to them about Sheryl being dead, but we never talked about how she died or why she died. Nor did we ever talk about why we hated Greg. And they never asked.

Yet they have to have known. People must have talked about this when they got older; it was a small town. They must have heard something.

NINE

We filed a wrongful death suit in August of 1992, primarily for the purpose of pursuing custody. Just like everything else surrounding Greg's murder of Sheryl, it was years before any results were seen.

My parents wanted to terminate his parental rights so they would never have to have to deal with Greg again. If we proved he murdered Sheryl in the civil case, we could use that in a custody case to do so. Another factor was our desire for him to not financially benefit from her death which he would do unless we prevailed in the wrongful death suit. If Roger wasn't going to pursue the investigation of her murder, we could do so in the civil wrongful death suit.

During this whole time there was little, if any, movement on the criminal case, at least not that we were made aware of. My parents had a meeting with Roger every year to see if there were any developments in the case. They never gave up. Roger made it a point to make them feel better during these meetings, at least at first, but as the years went on things began to seem hopeless.

Once the wrongful death suit was filed, Roger seemed content for us to pursue the criminal investigation. He was always cooperative and interested in what we were finding out, but there was no talk or movement toward charges and an arrest. I guess he was still waiting on someone to talk.

However, once I started scouring through Bob's files, I came upon some documents Roger turned over to us for the purpose of the wrongful death suit. He had reached out to Catherine J. MacMillan Sands, a professor at Central Washington University for an expert option. Ms. Sands reviewed the information Roger provided which was basically the same package he provided to the various other experts he consulted. When she replied with her opinion on June 1, 1994, reaching the same conclusion as everyone else—Sheryl's death was a homicide—she wrote something no one else had, at least officially. She wrote that she had several questions that she would like answers to and noted Roger may have many of the answers already. However, they were not included in the Crime Scene Report nor the Post-Mortem Report. She further stated: "I found both quite lacking as a matter of fact."

If I had been Roger and was confronted with such harsh written criticism, I'm not sure what I would have done. Perhaps nothing. Or perhaps it would have been what I needed to inspire me to hire the right experts and overcome the deficiencies in the medical examiner's report. This didn't happen.

Leonard Rumery was Roger's assistant state's attorney who succeeded him upon his retirement in 2000. If things were slow when Roger was in charge, they ground to a screeching halt when Leonard took over. The law was Leonard's second career. He first received a doctorate in conducting music in 1976. He played the recorder and other instruments for many years. He didn't turn to the law until 1989. I suspect Leonard's first career was his passion because he returned to that upon his retirement from the State's Attorney's Office in 2008.

My mom and dad met with Leonard when they could, but it wasn't even yearly anymore. Leonard was always nice, but they knew as soon as they left his office that he was not going to do anything to bring Greg to justice. The whole meeting would be him saying things such as, "So sorry for your loss. How are you doing? How are the boys?" He would appease them and send them on their way for another year.

There was a $12,000 reward for information that led to a conviction that was funded by my parents and others in the community. It was never touched. A few tips came in over the years, but nothing that ever amounted to anything that moved the investigation toward an arrest.

But at least we had the wrongful death suit so we could prove him guilty in a civil courtroom and to keep him from collecting the $50,000 Metropolitan life insurance policy he took out on her before her death. Also at stake were a $15,000 life insurance policy provided by her employer, and a $10,000 life insurance policy my dad took out on each one of us shortly after we were born and gave to us when we got married. Shortly after Sheryl's death we discovered that Greg had taken out this life insurance policy on her not long before he killed her.

Art and Bob put the insurance company on notice that we believed Greg was responsible for her death which would preclude him from collecting the money under the policy. Not knowing for sure who the money should legitimately be paid to, the insurance company paid the money to the court releasing themselves from liability and allowing interested parties to resolve who gets the money through litigation.

One of the greatest advantages of pursuing the wrongful death case was the opportunity to take depositions. I was allowed to sit in. I couldn't say anything because I wasn't a co-counsel so I had to sit there and listen to people say disparaging things about the case and my sister. It wasn't easy. My emotions were all over the place. At moments, I felt I was going to explode. When Les testified, I wanted to reach across the table and slap him. To this day, when I see Les and T-Byrd, it's almost as bad as when I see Greg. I want to hurt them.

I feel the same way about his parents. They had to have known what Greg did, and if Les and T-Byrd weren't involved, which they very well might have been, they knew what happened. Parents that raise children that can do these types of things, and the friends that enable despicable behavior are part of the problem. I think Greg's parents convinced themselves either he didn't do it or she deserved it. Either way, I hated them.

His grandmother, Lois, was different. She once saw my mother in a grocery store, took her hand, told her how sorry she was about Sheryl's death and how she was happy that she got custody of the kids. The word was she was abused by her husband, even to the point he would lock her in a tiny shed in their back yard for long periods of time to punish her. She knew it was true about Sheryl because she experienced abuse herself. It was ironic Greg chose to stay with them the night of the murder.

The expert witness testimony in the wrongful death suit clearly showed Sheryl did not commit suicide. Listening to the testimony, it was plain as day Greg murdered my sister. While it was validating to hear person after person be deposed and basically prove Greg was guilty, it also was difficult knowing that he continued to walk free.

Tim Byrd testified he decided to move to Wisconsin to work on his brother's farm and about the going away party the night before. Byrd said Greg seemed a bit down at the party, but he didn't know why. Byrd admitted he and Greg had in the past hid in the cornfield to spy on Sheryl to see if she was cheating on Greg. Byrd curiously testified he never asked Greg if he had anything to do with Sheryl's death and he and Greg had never discussed Sheryl's death at all, even though he has seen him about 200 times since it happened and, in theory, they are close friends.

Bobby Henderson, who was part of the Mansfield fire department and was one of the first people to arrive at the scene of Sheryl's death, was also deposed. He stated he saw Sheryl on the floor of the garage at the same time the rescue truck arrived with Greg on it. Henderson checked for signs of life but there were none. Greg asked him what was going on and Bobby told him to stay out of the garage as there was nothing to be done. Greg couldn't see Sheryl from where he was standing. He then broke down and started crying.

Lois Davis, Greg's grandmother, stated that Greg stayed at her house the night before Sheryl was found dead. He arrived at the home around 8 p.m. and didn't bring anything with him. The next time she saw him was around 6 a.m. the next day when he left the room he was staying in fully clothed. She testified Greg had not stayed at her home since he was a little boy and she hadn't invited him to stay. John Houser, Greg's dad, testified he took a change of clothes with him when he left to stay with his grandparents, which directly contradicted Lois.

Robert Mainit, Chief Deputy with Piatt County Sheriff's Office, testified he arrived at the house around 8 a.m. He later accompanied the body to Springfield Memorial Center where Grant Johnson, a pathologist licensed by the state, performed an autopsy to attempt to ascertain whether it was suicide or homicide. Mainit was asked his opinion and said he thought Sheryl had died 'at the hands of another person.'"

When asked why[2], he said "One piece of evidence that points-in my opinion points-in that direction was the tip of a rubber glove found in the rope around her neck". Sheryl was not wearing rubber gloves at the time of her death or when she was found.

He also testified, "I don't remember where the photos were but at one time I was shown some family photos and there was a picture of a deer that Greg Houser had shot or killed somehow and was hanging in the garage from the same pipe in that opening by a piece of yellow rope exactly what she was tied to…but the fact that it was common for

---

2. The following quotes initially contained grammar, spelling and punctuation errors that have now been corrected for easier reading and comprehension.

him to hang his deer in the garage form that pipe with that yellow rope and that's the way she was found."

And, "The fact there was no dirt on her feet...If her feet were clean how did she walk across the garage floor to that point and hang herself? And the fact he was still awaiting trial on the criminal sexual assault charge and there was a tremendous friction between the two. I personally felt that she did not commit suicide."

Others testified that Sheryl was happy and peaceful and excited about going forward with her life and that she was dedicated to her children.

Special agent Steven Hankel of the Illinois State Police stated no one within the Illinois State Police or the Piatt County Sheriff's Office has ever indicated they believed Sheryl's death was suicide. He also stated, in his opinion, Sheryl was dragged from one location to where she was found and she was probably already unconscious, if not already dead, when she was hung. He related that there were bruises to her neck that could not be connected to the rope wrapped around her neck.

At one point, Bob deposed the county coroner at the time[3], Dr. William Mundt, asking him:

"Dr Mundt. What, if anything, did you notice about the rope?"

Mundt replied, "Well, it was a weird knot, I know that."

"In what way was it weird?"

"Well, it was, at least twice, and I understand from the evidence later, it was three times doubled around the neck quite tight...and then it went into a very big knot, a very complex knot, then again it went to and over the pipe. And I noticed this very early on, that I didn't see it, say the lady threw herself off or fell off the step ladder, why it would stay where it was. I would have felt that, since the loop was just

---

3. This quote initially contained grammar, spelling and punctuation errors that have now been corrected for easier reading and comprehension.

over the pipe, and the pipe was very loose, why it wouldn't have gone quickly from one side or the other, therefore negating an attempt of suicide."

Deputy Dunlap testified he saw Lester Shores operating his motor vehicle a block away from where Greg's grandparents were and where Greg was sleeping. Les was alone. Five minutes later Dunlap again saw Les in his vehicle but this time he had a passenger with him. Who else could it have been but Greg?

Greg claimed under deposition, contrary to the testimony of his grandparents, that they asked him to spend the night with them.

There was much testimony that on the day of the death Greg didn't speak to anyone, not even his family or closest friends about Sheryl's death, how it had happened, and whether he believed it to be suicide. When he arrived at the scene, not once did he ask if something happened to Sheryl, or what happened. Not only that, but Greg, an EMT, wore gloves similar to the type of glove found at the scene.

Rod Englert testified the death was a homicide due to manual strangulation. He believed the body was moved from where it lay for a time then it was repositioned and attempted to be hung to make the scene appear to be a suicidal hanging.

His report in full is below.

Facts of the case are that on October 5, 1990 at approximately 7:30 a.m. Sheryl Houser was found deceased in her garage and the manner of death appeared to be a suicide by hanging. One of Sheryl Houser's children found Sheryl in the garage and subsequent to the discovery the police and emergency personnel responded to the scene. The medical examiner places the time of death around midnight.

It was learned that Sheryl Houser was a white female approximately 29 years of age estranged from her husband and with no history of suicidal tendencies.

Upon initial examination of the photos without having read any reports, the following observations were noted that appeared atypical of most suicides by hanging:

1)—The position of Houser's body relative to the floor. Her body was lower than what appears commonplace, although if this were the only unusual aspect of the case then it would not be remarkable.

2)—The ligature grooves about the neck are lateral which is common to ligature strangulations in homicides, whereas in suicides the angle of the ligature grooves go upward and are very close to the earlobes.

3)—A preliminary row of furrows on Houser's neck are lateral and then what appears to be a secondary position of the rope appears at the base of her skull. Refer to photo # SA 32. This is atypical of suicides by hanging and appears that the ligature was applied tightly by other than Sheryl Houser. She was then suspended to make the scene appear to be a suicide.

4)—In the photos of Houser's neck there appear to be contusions below her mandible on both sides of her neck consistent with marks made by throttling of her neck by another person's hand. These marks are consistent with manual strangulation and inconsistent with suicidal ligature strangulation.

Refer to photos 19, 20 and 22. There are what appear to be contusions consistent with throttling in the frontal area of the neck below the lowest ligature groove, and again, these contusions appear to be from throttling as opposed to self—inflicted ligature strangulation. Refer to photo (sic).

5)—Abrasions on the victim's extremities (elbow, legs, and feet) as noted in the photos 26, 24, 4, 27, 28, and autopsy report indicate a struggle. Consistent with that opinion is the fact that not only is the garment tag from Houser's night gown (sic) caught in the rope around her neck, but her short head hair is also mixed in with layers of the rope. Refer to photog 8, 9, 13, and SA 32.

6)—What appears to be an unusual amount of hairs on Houser's night gown (sic) is suspicious and consistent with a struggle. If any of the hairs were closely examined, hair roots present would give further indication of a struggle by the victim at the hands of a second party. Refer to photos SA 32, 33, and 38.

7)—In photo SA 32 I was informed that the foreign object clinging to and entwined in the knot at the base of the skull is a particle of rubber glove. There was also a like particle of latex from a glove on the floor next to a leg of the ladder in photo SA 15. Again, if another person was trying to subdue or overcome resistance by Sheryl Houser the particles of gloving would be consistent with such an event as opposed to suicidal ligature strangulation, which if so in this case would be unexplainable due to the absence of gloves about the victim.

8)—Houser in photo has blood on her left night gown (sic) strap consistent with her position as found. What appears to be blood on this garment at the area of the left knee is inconsistent with her position as found or any other position in suicidal hangings. The 90 0 drop of blood means it dropped perpendicular to the surface of the gown as opposed to an angular drop. The source of the blood would be from her mouth or nasal passages with her head and body bent over toward her knees in order for the blood to land at 90 (sic). An angular drop is elongated and the more acute the angle, the more the elongation. It is not conceivable Sheryl Houser would or could have placed herself in such a position by self—inflicted ligature hanging. If the garment is still in evidence the blood should be examined to determine if it is in fact Sheryl Houser's and whether this drop was present at the scene. It is not visible in crime scene photos.

What appears to be blood on the right chest area of Houser is inconsistent with the scene unless that blood stain was the result of her head resting on her right side and then the body repositioned by someone else. Refer to photo # SA 31. The stain is very faint and possibly not blood but should be examined further.

In photo # SA 26 there is what appears to be a soiled area on the night gown (sic) indicating contact in a wiping or swiping motion on a dirty surface such as the floor. Again, this would be consistent with a struggle involving another party.

10)—Information was also received from State's Attorney Simpson that in photo #12 the lividity pattern on Houser's back is not from the autopsy table but consistent with an object with a similar pattern in the garage. Houser's position when found had no object under her upper back nor was this portion of her back touching the floor according to the photos. This means Houser lay in another position after death and was moved after lividity fixed enough to leave the pattern on her back. Also, a point which is noted as unusual is the absence of blanched marks on the buttocks of Houser in photos #12, 24, and 33. It appears that in the position she was found, and if death occurred as a result of being self—inflicted, there would have been the presence of white areas in dependent zones on the portion of buttocks making contact with the cement floor. Again, the absence of same is consistent with Houser being murdered, her body laying for quite some time allowing lividity to fix, then being repositioned to make it appear she committed suicide. A forensic medical examiner should be consulted for an expert opinion on the information regarding lividity.

11)—Small abrasions on the outside portion of Houser's right foot have debris or a foreign particle clinging to the wound. This is consistent with having been in a struggle and resisting force against her. It is not consistent with self—inflicted hanging.

12)—Other findings which are suspicious in nature but certainly not evidentiary is (sic) the 3 loops around Houser's neck with the rope. I 'm told the FBI lab in Washington, D.C. has an expert on knots and ropes, and it is suggested a rope expert examine the slip knot to determine if the application *is one that could have been done by Houser or is consistent with wraps done by another party.*

13)—It should be noted that it is not that common for women to hang themselves, as opposed to other options Sheryl Houser could have chosen, such as overdose, because she was a nurse.

My preliminary opinion at this point is based upon the limited information received, and until additional information, if any, is brought to my attention, it is my opinion Sheryl Houser's death was not self—inflicted. This appears to be a homicide of manual strangulation by throttling with the hands in addition to a ligature application of the rope. Her body was moved from where she lay for a period of time allowing lividity to settle or fix. Then she was repositioned and hung up to make the scene appear a suicidal hanging.

In February of 1996, after the depositions, Greg's attorney moved for summary judgment, asking the judge to dismiss the case as the evidence discovered so far in the case did not support a conclusion that Greg murdered Sheryl. As Bob was preparing his response to Greg's motion for summary judgment, he sent me a copy, in the closing paragraph of his letter he wrote: "As a final note, I simply want to tell you that after having spent more than 35 additional hours preparing this response and having reviewed all of the material which has been obtained and generated to date, I am even more firmly convinced than I was earlier that Greg with or without the help from others killed Sheryl. I remain committed to doing my very best to help you. I only hope that my very best will bring justice and closure."

The summary judgment was denied, and the case was headed to trial. In January of 1997, out of the blue, Hayes wrote Bob exploring settlement of the wrongful death case.

Bob immediately replied to Hayes' inquiry, telling him that exploring settlement would impede his trial preparation and his clients (my parents) weren't interested in that. We were not going to let an opportunity to get justice for Sheryl pass us by, even if it was to be in a civil courtroom. It wouldn't be as gratifying as a criminal conviction and a prison sentence, but at least there wouldn't be any doubt she did not commit suicide.

Bob and I met with my parents. We had serious issues to consider. If Mom and Dad settled the wrongful death suit, there would be no termination of Greg's parental rights. He would not agree to that. However, he would relinquish all claim to the life insurance monies and her pension fund and the costs of litigation would be over.

While we wanted to fight and Bob was confidently willing to do so on our behalf, we were tired. We had met our primary objective which was my parents having permanent custody of the boys. While they would still have to visit Greg, he was not responsible for their day-to-day care. In other words, they would not be raised by the monster who brutally killed their mother and left her for her beloved little boys to find. While the decision wasn't made quickly and it wasn't made without carefully weighing many times the pros and the cons of settlement, we all knew it was time to settle the case, put the money in trust for the boys' college educations, and move on.

After the case was settled, I cried alone at home. I felt like I had once again failed my sister. But I had to look out for my parents and the boys. My mom couldn't emotionally handle a trial and I didn't know how my dad would pay for the cost of trial preparation.

Someday I vowed to make it up to Sheryl. I would never lose hope.

TEN

Then, for the longest time, nothing happened. While we never completely gave up hope, we certainly were not overly optimistic anymore. The days had turned to months, then years, and then we were measuring time in decades since Greg had killed my sister. And still he walked free.

Life moved on for us all, including myself. In September of 1996, I gave birth to my son, Alexander. I spent much of my maternity leave watching the trial of O.J. Simpson for the murder of his wife, Nicole, and her friend, Ron Goldman. This might not have been the best choice as it brought up numerous issues for me. The trial began on January 24, 1995, seven months after the murders, and was televised for 134 days. On October 3, 1995, at 10:00, I turned on the TV to hear the verdict.

I was stunned. O.J being found not guilty hurt way more than it should have. It was almost as if Greg had been tried and acquitted.

I couldn't believe O.J was going free. Of course, OJ had killed Nicole, just like Greg had killed Sheryl. It was obvious. My mind began to go to some dark places. Perhaps it was a good thing Roger hadn't tried Sheryl's case because Greg might have been acquitted, gotten the boys, raised them to be monsters, and the cycle of violence would have been repeated over and over and over.

John and I moved to Spruce Creek in Daytona Beach. It was a fly-in community that surrounded an old military runway. The houses backed up to taxiways and large hangars for airplanes were attached like garages to people's homes. John thought he had died and gone to heaven. We bought a peach stucco three-bedroom home with a white tile roof. It was perfect for us. John became unemployed briefly then founded Ashworth Aviation and began doing contract maintenance at Sanford Airport which led to work flying a corporate jet.

While I was away on a trip with a close female friend, I called John to say hello. To my surprise, he told me he had been offered a job flying for a large paper company out of St. Louis and he accepted it. He would be gone by the time I returned. He planned to live with a friend while I stayed behind, worked my job, took care of our son, and figured out the process of selling the house. I was surprised he accepted the job without talking to me but I never said a word. It took me 9 months to sell the house and join John in the spring of 1998, in a home he purchased without me even seeing it. Again, I said nothing. At least I was finally moving closer to home which I had wanted for a long time.

Alexander and I had barely been in St. Louis a year when John's company merged with one based in Chicago. John was advised that the St. Louis operation would be shut down. He was without a job again. He called a large insurance company in Bloomington, Illinois to see if they were hiring in-house pilots. By chance, they had purchased new jets but didn't have pilots type-rated to fly them and there was a waiting list for the training. As luck would have it, the jets they bought were the same type John had been flying for the paper company.

For the first time in a long time, I thought that perhaps my luck was changing. We could move to Bloomington only 30 miles from where we grew up. I got a job working as an attorney for an insurance company. Before long, we had our second child, who we named Mickael.

While I really enjoyed being home and close to family, I'm not so sure John did. The demons he seemed to have left behind when we moved to Florida started to haunt him again.

He was gone often, taking numerous trips without us, and raced his motorcycle all day Sunday. If the kids and I wanted to spend time with him on the weekend, I had to pack us up and tag along to the track for the day. It was a lot of work and it consumed an entire day of my weekend.

While I hadn't lost all hope when it came to Sheryl, life was moving on. I was busy raising two children virtually on my own as John was so often gone on work trips and I too was working full time and traveling. I was defending class action lawsuits on behalf of the company I was working for, traveling coast to coast.

Mom and Dad were nearly as busy as I was with raising their second set of children. The boys graduated from high school in 2003, 2005 and 2007. All proceeded to go to college using the money that had been held in trust to pay for nearly all of their college educations. My dad told me that when his friends asked why he didn't own more farmland he replied that he had paid for seven college educations which allowed seven children to be financially independent so he thought it was just as good if not a better investment than growing his farm.

Little did we know we had a strong advocate on our side we weren't aware of yet. Dana Rhodes was in college at Illinois State University in October of 1990 when Sheryl was murdered. At the time, she saw news coverage and heard a lot of community discussion surrounding Sheryl's death. Her mother told her at the time that there was "no way" it was a suicide. Dana never forgot that, and the case never left her mind. Dana went on to law school and began practicing law in her hometown of Monticello, Illinois, in 1997.

When Leonard announced his retirement, his assistant, Gary A. Webber, announced his intention to run for State's

Attorney. Dana made the decision to run also. Upon announcing her candidacy, she stated that she was running for office because the current state's attorney had been lenient on criminals and was quoted as saying, "I decided to run for state's attorney after conversing with law enforcement. There needs to be more of a focus on prosecuting felony cases." She pointed out that from 2001 to 2007, the Piatt County prosecutor had much lower rate of felony convictions when compared with similar counties.

Dana won and was appointed in November of 2008.

One of the first things she did when elected was meet with members of the Illinois State Police for an update on Sheryl's case. Later, she began meeting with Special Agent Chad Dumonceaux and Special Agent Rodney Slayback and developed a close working relationship with them as they shared her passion to pursue and obtain a conviction for murder.

I heard from Dana at different times over the years. She was clear that she was going to push for Greg to face justice and she wasn't going to give up. Still, I took this with a grain of salt. While I was impressed with Dana, this wasn't totally new to me. Over the years, every once in a while, someone involved with law enforcement would call me and give me some information just so I knew they hadn't totally stopped trying. This happened at least 5 times. Then I called my sisters and we discussed whether we should tell Mom and Dad about this so-called "new movement" in the case.

If we told our parents, Mom would be excited and hopeful; she wanted justice for Sheryl more than anything in the world. Dad would be worried and stressed because he knew what it would do to our mother if nothing happened yet again or, worse yet, something happened and we lost. The first few times we heard such news, we let them know something positive might be going on in the investigation. Then, when nothing happened, my mother would get sad and depressed. Eventually we just decided not to tell her about any so-called good news. What was the use?

My marriage wasn't perfect but I accepted it. While he didn't give me all I needed, I never complained or asked for more. I believed in marriage and living up to my vows. I had mentally prepared myself for a call from someone about him dying in a plane crash and how I would cope with such news as his flying worried me. However, I never in my wildest dreams prepared myself for what happened.

John woke up one morning the week before Thanksgiving, kissed me goodbye, and left for "deer camp", an annual hunting trip in Southern Illinois. I stayed home to work and take care of kids as usual. One night after work, I was sifting through the mail and found a notice from our bank that seemed unusual. It said the address on our bank accounts had been changed and advised that if I had not made the changes I should call the fraud department immediately, which I did. What I heard was unexpected and shocking, "Ma'am, your husband, John, changed the addresses on these accounts earlier in the week, you'll have to talk to him."

I had no idea what was happening or why he would have done that. I called him; there was no answer. I checked our bank accounts online. Fifteen thousand dollars that had been in one of our savings accounts was gone. I started to panic. I must have called him 20 times.

Finally, I got ahold of him. What he said left me speechless. "I'm leaving you. I'm not coming back." Then he hung up.

I called my sister, Lisa, told her what had just happened and asked her to please come get the kids. I tried calling him again. No answer.

I called his mother and told her what I knew and asked her if she knew what was going on. She was as stunned and shocked as me.

I couldn't function or think straight. I couldn't get ahold of him. All I could do was wait for him to call or walk through the door. Finally, Sunday night he called and said he would come by and talk to me. He did, but he offered no further explanation. I was devastated and couldn't understand what was happening or why.

I didn't get out of bed the entire week of Thanksgiving. Finally, my dad looked at me and said, "Life's a bitch, kid, then you die. You better get it together. You have two kids to take care of."

Hearing this from him didn't upset me. I knew exactly what he meant. It is probably exactly what he told himself after Sheryl was murdered and he found himself raising a second set of children in his 50s.

In the coming weeks, I went to work every day and then came home to sit on the floor, lean against the wall in our bedroom, and cry. The kids would come in and look at me with scared and worried eyes. Then I pulled myself together and made supper for them before we all went to bed together in the same bed.

A few days before Christmas, it hit me like a brick. He was having an affair. I knew John well enough to know he wasn't doing this on his own. He wasn't strong enough for that. I had always given him the love and support he needed and now I wasn't giving him any. Someone else must have been providing that to him.

I called him. It was late. This time he answered. I point blank asked him, "Are you having an affair?"

He didn't answer. He didn't say anything. I asked a few more times, then said, "I know you are or otherwise you would have answered. I demand to know who."

He wouldn't tell me. I demanded several more times. Finally, he said that I knew her. That just made me demand to know more. After more games, he finally told me it was the lady who cut his hair, Amena.

I was furious. He had asked me to allow this woman to give Mickael her first haircut. Like the idiot I was when it came to John, I didn't ask any questions. I made the appointment and went. I introduced myself, put Mickael in the chair, took a video, and made small talk. I thought she looked at me strangely and acted weird. Now I know why. She was sleeping with my husband. How could he have done that to me? Why would he have put me in that situation?

I was mad and disgusted. I wanted to know if he had sex with her in our bed. He wouldn't answer which was a sure sign that he did. I wanted to throw up. After I hung up, I went through the house, grabbed all of his things, and threw them in the garage.

I was as mad at myself as I was at him. How could I have been so naïve? How could I have been such an idiot? The signs had all been there. He was distant. He accused me of having an affair out of the blue one night. He stopped coming to the kids' sporting events. He was gone even on the days he wasn't flying. The list goes on.

I found out the day he left our home he moved in with Amena without a second thought. They had been planning their departures together. She was on her second husband at the time and had two little girls with two different fathers.

I needed my parents' support badly, but again they just weren't available to me in the way I needed. They tried. They just couldn't do it. If it weren't for my sisters, especially Lisa, I'm not sure what I would have done or if I would have survived.

John leaving cut me so deeply I didn't know if I could survive. It wasn't what he did to me as a wife. It was what he did to me as my best friend. I had been there for him. I picked him up when he was down. I supported him and his dreams, career, interests, and hobbies every step of the way and this is how he repaid me.

To this day, I still don't understand it and probably never will. I just hope and pray that my inability to cope for so long didn't permanently impact my beloved children.

We divorced quickly. There was no need to delay matters when he was already living with another woman. With the help of my family, an amazing group of friends, and a counselor that I still meet with today, I managed to get it together enough to start a new life for me and the kids.

In February of 2006, I began getting calls from a doctor's office looking for John. It irritated me. I had always taken care of everything for him and it was obvious that without me notifying people of his new contact information, it wasn't getting done. I stopped taking the calls and never said a word to John. He could figure it out on his own. Or Amena could figure it out for him.

Within a few weeks, John called and said that he needed to tell me something. I wasn't interested but I listened. He had been diagnosed with cancer. This sent me back into a tailspin. I still loved him but had been trying very hard to dissolve the glue between us. Now he was back at my doorstep inviting me back into his life. I jumped in with both feet. I went to his doctor's appointments along with Amena. She and I were on each side of John when a doctor told him that he had esophageal cancer that had metastatized to his liver and was stage 4. The doctor recommended that he get his affairs in order because he only had 6 months to live. We buried him 5 ½ months later in August 2006.

I begged him to leave Amena and come back home so I could take care of him and he could be with the kids. I begged him to remarry me so he could die with his family by his side. He refused. I had to take the kids to his and Amena's house to visit. I made him meals, visited him with the kids, and acted as much as possible as if we had never divorced. Amena finally told John she didn't want me in her house anymore so I sat on their front step while the kids visited. Eventually, he called his sister and asked her and his parents to move him out of Amena's house and into his parents' home. The kids and I visited often. I implored him to get his affairs in order. To leave what he had received in our divorce to the kids. I told him that he didn't have to leave it to me. I asked him to make the kids the beneficiary of his rather large life insurance policy. I wouldn't touch the money; it could be to fund their college educations. To me, that was only fair because we split their college funds we had saved so far in the divorce and didn't leave those funds intact for them. He wouldn't do it.

I had suffered a tragic loss of a loved one before without any warning. This time there was warning. This time there was time to make things right. To say things and do things in anticipation of dying. I bought him two books that were meant for a dying person to fill out and leave his children. I wanted him so badly to leave notes and letters and messages to them. I wanted him to do the things that I know Sheryl would have done for her boys had she been given the time. He had the time and he wouldn't do it. I was beyond crushed again.

I am a fixer. I wanted to fix Sheryl, her marriage, her problems, and the aftermath. I wanted to fix John after the death of Kris. I thought I did but now I know I didn't have the ability to do that. John, like all of us, had to fix himself. I didn't cause his issues and I couldn't solve them, as hard as I tried.

Before he died, John said to me, "It must have been part of God's plan for me to have an affair and leave you so that when I got cancer and died you would be prepared to live without me."

I'll go to my grave without forgetting this because it was so hurtful. I think about this statement differently now because I have such a greater understanding of myself and life in general—even on his death bed, it was all about John.

In April of 2011, I was at work when my mom called. She rarely called during the day so I knew it was important.

She told me that Bob died. I was shocked. Bob was only 54 and had died of a massive heart attack.

There were so many things I wanted to say to him and never did. I wanted to tell him from the bottom of my heart how much I appreciated him and all the work he had done for us. I wanted him to know that without him, I'm not sure what would have happened to the boys. And most of all, I wanted to hug him. The work he and I had done all those years had been done long distance and over the phone. I had never given him a hug.

By this time, I was two years into a new relationship which seemed promising. Alexander became Facebook friends with two brothers in Farmer City who raced four wheelers. Their dad was single, and Alexander thought we might get along because we could go to races together. I had continued Alexander's motorcycle racing career after John died. Every Sunday, I packed up him, his motorcycle, Mickael, and our Italian Greyhound named Johnny and we went to the races.

When he told me it was Joe Plunk I smiled. Of all people, Joe was a close friend of Sheryl's who had been married to a close friend of my sister, Lisa. Joe had been hauling beans the day of Sheryl's murder and had to drive by her house multiple times. Joe and his wife, Jenny, were some of my family's biggest supporters. Joe and Jenny spent hours tracking down information for the police and for me. They did everything they could to bring Greg to justice and support my family. Now Joe was to be reintroduced to me in a whole new light. Perhaps Sheryl had something to do with that.

ELEVEN

In 2011, Dana engaged Dr. Scott Denton, a well-respected forensic pathologist, to do a complete review of the evidence in Sheryl's case. His conclusion, like all but the original pathologists who studied the case, was that the cause of death was a homicide made to look like a suicide.

Dr. Denton's report was instrumental in moving the case forward. Dana now had a respected, forensic pathologist's thorough review of the evidence and his opinion. And she was going to use it.

After reviewing Dr. Denton's review and report, Dana called my sister, Julie. Julie and her husband and three children lived in Monticello where Dana lived. They had children the same ages and ran in some of the same social circles. Dana felt confident enough to tell Julie that they hadn't given up on the case and were looking into it again. Julie mentioned this call to Lisa and me. We were optimistic but we decided at this point against saying a word to Mom and Dad. There was no need to get their hopes up only to be shattered again for what seemed like the hundredth time.

The police were closing in and working the case. They even called Greg in for an interview. What follows are excerpts from a police interview[4] that was done by Chad Dumonceaus and Michael Campbell of the Illinois State Police.

---

4. This interview contains grammar, spelling and punctuation errors that have not been corrected.

CD: Yep, yep. It's been 25 years. Do you remember the events kind of leading up to that? Kinda walk me through.

GH: We were going through a divorce. It was going to be a horrible, probably—not a simple custody battle.

CD: Yep.

GH: And, um...her parents were horrible towards me and were pretty much in the middle of things. And it just wasn't gonna reconcile.

CD: Yeah.

GH: And, I think at that time, excuse me, I'm dry-mouthed, but I think...it seemed like we were splitting the residency. Like I was there three days, she was there three days, back and forth for the kids. And it was her weekend. I was on the fire department. I stayed at my grandparents' that night. Friday was the night that...or Friday was the day I was off. And, we got a rescue call that morning and it was to the house and I probably shouldn't have went but I drove the truck 'cause I was around and that's when we found her.

CD: Okay, okay, so you were off work that day?

GH: On Friday, yes.

CD: But you still went in? You went to work? Or why were...What truck did you drive and why were you at work?

GH: Firetruck.

CD: You drove the firetruck.

GH: I was actually with my grandparents and they were like, a couple blocks from the fire house, so...

CD: Okay, alright, let's kind of go back a little bit. You said it wasn't going very good. the relationship...

GH: No one wants divorce.

CD: Alright, so I'm gonna kinda go back here a little bit. Like I said, I read the case, I read the reports, this, that, and the other. And so, it sounds like you and Sheryl had a little history between the two of you, as far as maybe some physical contact that might be seen as...

GH: We didn't beat each other up, if that's what you're asking.

CD: Right, well, I just, I am asking...

GH: I went, I went to jail once because she started to do something and I went like that. And that was as hard as I grabbed her. The officer told me that that was battery and I went to jail.

CD: Okay.

GH: I admitted it. I did not grab her, I did not hit her, nothing like that.

CD: Okay. And then fast forward about a month later, there's the accusation that...the sex assault thing. That you held her down with a yellow rope.

GH: Yeah.

CD: Yeah, what about that one?

GH: That was bullshit.

CD: *That something that happened or no?*

GH: *That was bullshit. No, that was not something that happened.*

CD: *What about all the marks she had on her lips, and face, and her neck, and stuff?*

GH: *I don't know where they come from. They didn't come from me.*

CD: *Okay. So, when we first started your interview, Greg, um, I informed you that the case had been reviewed.*

GH: *Uh huh.*

CD: *And the case was ruled a homicide, meaning she didn't do what she did to herself.*

GH: *Uh huh.*

CD: *Are you aware of how she died?*

GH: *Yeah.*

CD: *What is your knowledge?*

GH: *She hung herself.*

CD: *Okay, well, I'm here to tell you that's not true.*

GH: *Okay.*

CD: *And that you're not even flinching over that. She was strangled to death.*

GH: *And you think I did it.*

CD: *I don't know who did it. That's why we're sitting here talking to you. All I know is that you were her husband at the time.*

CD: *And part of this case is that sex assault, the battery, everything leading up to her death. Okay? There is a chain, there's a history of events between you and her. And that yellow rope kinda is similar to markings that would have been, that would have caused, those abrasions on her lip, the swelling, and you know, that kind of coincide with what she told the police officers 25 years ago. And then we find her, less than a month to the day, hanging by a yellow nylon rope with the same type of abrasions seen on her neck that are inconsistent with a suicide by hanging.*

GH: *I don't know.*

CD: *Do you see, do you see why we're going through this, why we're sitting here?*

GH: *Yes.*

CD: *Okay.*

GH: *But I don't have an answer for you.*

CD: *Okay, and you're, just so I'm understanding what was written 25 years ago, your primary means of birth control, you already had three kids...*

GH: *She was Catholic.*

CD: *She was Catholic. Okay, so you guys didn't use birth control then? Or you did? Cause, I think in your interview...*

GH: *Condoms once in a while. She had... what in the hell is it called diaphragm. She had one of those for a while. So that every time you had a kid you had to get it re-sized. She hadn't done that yet.*

CD: Well, I want to tell you that in that crime scene, we found, well, not me because I was only about 8 years old. A condom was found, Greg. And you know what was in that condom? Your DNA. And her DNA. A fresh condom was found at the crime scene where your wife was not suicidal and hung herself, but was manually strangulated, by hands or a rope. And your DNA is there in a condom.

GH: And I'm telling you, I didn't do it.

CD: You didn't do what?

GH: I did not kill my wife. Now, where the condom come from, I don't know.

CD: So, she was a nurse for 6 years. She's a cleaning lady. Well, not...she's a clean lady. Nurses by habit are kind of clean.

GH: I don't know where they found it at.

CD: Right. She's got three kids. You already told me your one year old is crawling around, getting into stuff. You've got a three year old and a five year old running around the house. And there's a used condom on the floor that's somewhat fresh and it has your sperm in it...your DNA. And you just told me you hadn't been with her for almost 30 days. You expect me to think she's...

GH: I don't know where you found it.

CD: ...going to have a used condom laying on the floor when she's got three boys running around? And the day she's found dead, there's a condom. And like I told you, it's been 25 years. Things have changed. Technology has changed. And that DNA came back to you, Greg.

GH: I took a DNA test as soon as...

CD: I know you did. And here we are, 25 years later, and they can take that condom that we have in evidence still, along with everything else, and submit it to the lab. And you know what? We found your DNA in that condom, Greg. Explain that one to me.

GH: I don't know where you found it. I don't know.

CD: We found it in the house.

GH: Where?

CD: It was a walking path. So you mean to tell me you don't know how your condom with your sperm and DNA got in the house?

GH: I do not.

CD: So how's a nurse of six years with three boys walking around the house going to leave a condom laying on the floor? She's not.

GH: I don't have a answer for you.

CD: She's not. So, I don't, I don't think that you meant for her to get hurt that night. But I do think that you were there. I think you made your way over there after T-Byrd's party at some point in the evening, to try to make up, to try to talk to her, to have a casual conversation with her. Just to try to get things back on track, possibly. And I think things got a little out of hand. Whether...and I think you guys probably had sex, you know what, she was probably trying to get back on board, too. Because she does have the three boys. And let's face it, boys need a father in their life. And you were their father.

Most women don't want somebody else raising their kids. They want the biological father raising their kids. And that was you. And I'll be damned if she probably, even though she was telling other people all this, that, and the other you know, whatever she was saying about you. You know, deep down, she probably...you were her husband of eight years, you said? And I don't doubt for an instance that she probably wanted, at some point, to stay with you and help raise those kids. Cause you were their dad, darn it. And you what? You didn't get to raise those kids because of all of this. And I don't think you went over there and I don't think she and you meant to have anything bad happen. But I think things got a little out of control, like they have on previous incidences, where you guys got in an argument, things get out of hand, and activities some happened that hurt somebody. And I think she got hurt badly that night, you didn't know what to do about it, said "oh crap," let's work this out, and one thing led to another and she was put in the position she was put in. You didn't mean for her to get hurt that night, did you?

GH: I wasn't out there that night. I'm telling you straight up, I was not out there. I was with my grandparents.

CD: Okay. Well, we talked to your grandparents too, as you know, okay? And they can't confirm your story, Greg. But what does confirm your story, or what doesn't confirm your story is that fact that your used condom, your freshly used condom, is in the house that night. So, you were over there and you guys had some sex, consensual or maybe not so much, she was probably trying to work things out, let you in, maybe just to see how things roll, you know, it's an emotional event, I get it, like I said, one thing led to another, maybe she wanted to stop it...

CD: *I was not out there.*

GH: *I was not out there.*

CD: *Well, your condom was out there, Greg. And your DNA is out there.*

GH: *I don't know where that come from. And I was not there.*

CD: *Okay. So, the condom that's out there that has your DNA in it came from only you. Okay?*

GH: *Mmm hmm.*

CD: *So, I would really appreciate it if you could look at me, man to man, and just say "you know what, I did not want her to get hurt." I get that, I understand that...*

GH: *I'm lookin' at you right now and telling you, I was not out there.*

CD: *Who was out there then?*

GH: *I don't know. I was not out there.*

CD: *Okay. So, she was hung up in the same fashion, somewhat, like hanging a deer, in a garage that belonged to you and her. She'd been scared to death of you. She changed all her locks. The lights were all turned off. You went over there, I think. You guys had some...some sort of conversation. Things got a little out of hand, one thing led to another, you guys ended up having relations. Condom got left behind, okay? I'll tell you…she was…she did not hang herself, Greg. Do you understand that?*

GH: I didn't see the crime scene. I don't…

CD: Do you understand…

GH: Yes, I understand what you're telling me.

CD: Okay. You know what…

GH: I was not there.

CD: You know what else was at the crime scene? Rubber glove tips that were stuck in the knots around her neck. She wasn't wearing rubber gloves when she was found. But the person that tied her up had rubber gloves on. Cause they were trying to protect their DNA, their fingerprints, this, that, and the other. And you know what we found in that rope? A piece of a rubber glove, stuck in the knot on her neck. And we found your condom on the crime scene, in the crime scene. Part of the crime scene where a female, your wife, the mother of your children, was found. Killed. Not suicide. Killed. And you sit here and you want me to understand that somehow your used condom from you got in that house by somebody else? There's only one person that put that condom there. There's only one person that could have worn that condom and had their semen in that condom. And that one person is you, Greg. You're the only person that could have put that condom there…okay?

GH: I'm telling you, I don't know how it got there.

CD: Now your boys went most of their life without a father, right? You told me you didn't really have a relationship with them. You know where they are. You probably follow with their activities, right?

GH: Mmm hmmm.

CD: And now is your chance to explain to them, yes, I was there. I did not mean for your mom to get hurt.

GH: I'm telling you I wasn't there.

CD: And there's no way—you're catching that arrow right now. You're not deflecting anywhere else, okay. And we're throwing arrows at other people right now. We're throwing arrows at Lester. We're throwing arrows at Tim Byrd, okay? And all these other people you said. There is someone you worked with at Southland that said you had a conversation after one of your arguments and you said "I should just string her up like a deer. And, you know what, we found her strung up like a deer in your garage at a time when no one can vouch where you were and with evidence of science 25 years later put you there at a time when you said you were not there.

GH: I was not there. And that comment was never made. Who, who made that comment?

CD: It's in the report from 1990 from one of your co-workers.

GH: No.

CD: Cause you hunted, you strung deer up, you know how to do that, okay? She was your wife. Strangling somebody takes a lot of force. It's very personal. You are right there in their personal space. It's not somebody that gets off the interstate that strangles somebody. That doesn't happen. Those are stabbings or shootings. People don't go into somebody's house, who have just changed their locks because they're scared to death of their husband, and get strangled by a stranger, okay? These things come from home. We know Tim was sweet on her, we know Lester might have had the hots for her, we don't know if he was sweet for her or not. But you're catching the arrow pretty big right now, Greg.

GH: I understand that.

CD: So, from 10:45, 10:30 pm, which you told the investigators in 1990, until 7:00 am, you never left grandma and grandpa's house. Except to go eat breakfast at mom and dad's.

GH: I don't remember about breakfast, to tell you the truth. That was 25 years ago. I remember spending the night with my grandparents. I don't know if I went home and ate breakfast at my mom and dad's or not.

CD: So, do you remember wrapping your arms, or your hands around her neck and strangling her to death?

GH:

CD: Do you remember wrapping a rope around her neck and hanging her up like she was a deer?

GH: Didn't do that.

CD: Then who did?

GH: I didn't do it. I don't know.

CD: Which one of your friends' DNA is going to be on the nightgown? Lester's or Tim's or is it yours?

GH: I don't know.

CD: It's gotta be one of them, right? Whose do you think it is, if it's not yours?

GH: We gonna do this all night?

MC: What we've talked about all evening long. Where all of these unanswered questions end.

GH: Mm hmm.

MC: They end with you. The person who had motive, who had means. You had ways to get out to your house. If you would have knocked on your door at 1:00 or 2:00 in the morning, she'd have been pissed, but she'd have opened the door. If for no other reason to not wake the kids up. To see what you wanted. And you had opportunity, because between 8:30 and 7:00 something the next morning, you're at your grandparents' house, who had no line of sight to your bedroom and were extremely hard of hearing. So, you could have got up and walked out of the house and they would have never been the wiser. Plus, you put the condom, and your history, you put all of that...where does it point? And people are going to ask what has he done in the last 25 years to find answers for himself? Nothing. What has his answer to every question been? "Wasn't me, wasn't there." Are those answers going to change when the DNA comes back? Are those answers going to change even if it comes back to one of your buddies who you may have had suspicions of? But never had the guts to put it on the table? The kids are going to ask those questions. And, believe it or not, I believe it from my parents that you never stop being a parent. Doesn't matter if your kids are 8, 18, 28, 58, doesn't matter. You never stop being a parent. And if for no other reason, this is a parenting moment. This is your opportunity, as we've said time and time again, to say whatever it is you need to say. Because your kids can understand if you went over there to work it out. Maybe you had a come to Jesus meeting that night and you said I'm going to go talk to Sheryl because I want to work this out once and for all, be part of a family. I want my family back. When you went out there, she let you in, the arguments ensued, and something happened. They can understand that. Or, you can not say a word and let your kids believe you're a cold-blooded killer. Because it doesn't matter if it was you or Tim Byrd, or Lester Shores, or whoever. You can't tell me in Mansfield that someone can do this and you not know, in your heart of hearts, and not lift a finger to do anything about it. Is that the legacy you want to leave your kids? Because, you do that and you'll write off any chance you have of a relationship. I don't think that's what you want. I really don't. I think you want a relationship with your boys. But I think a hurdle that you can't overcome is telling them what really happened. I think it scares the hell out of you. I think, I think this, you know like we said before, even knowing and not doing anything is the same as doing it yourself. And that's a lot to let go of. But if you want a relationship with your kids, it's what you're going to have to do. And they deserve that. I mean, you have your opinion about your in-laws, their grandparents, all you want. But even if you take them out of the mix, they've had a rough life. For all intents and purposes, they've grown up without a mom. And after October 5th, they've grown up without a dad. And it's really never too late. You said before, you don't know where to start.

GH: You're talking about with my kids?

MC: Yeah.

GH: Doesn't really make any difference at this point what I say, you're not believing anything.

MC: Well, right now what I believe doesn't matter. Cause I don't think you're going to tell me. So, it's up to you how your kids find out. Cause like I said, they're going to know. They're all adults. They're going to know every detail of what happened that night. And I have never spoken a word to any of them. But when that day comes, I'm sure they're going to make up their own minds. And I don't think they want to believe the worst, but what choice are they going to have? And you don't want them to think of you that way.

GH: I'm going to say it again. I wasn't out there. I don't know of anybody that was. I did not hurt her. I did not kill her. That's just the fact right there. I wasn't there. I don't know how many times I can keep saying that. How that got there, I don't know. I don't know.

MC: You've said 4 times since we met if you were, you've asked us if you're being charged. You think you're going to be?

GH: I don't know.

MC: It's obviously a concern of yours, right?

GH: Well, wouldn't it be everybody's?

MC: If I had absolutely nothing to do with anything and after 25 years, two investigators showed up and said we're looking at your former wife's murder. And you asked us, before we even left, are you being charged. It wasn't "well, it's about damn time." Isn't 'I've been waiting for this day for a long time." None of that reaction. It's "am I being charged?" Again, as we talked about before, none of which is normal. Normal is to be relieved, cautiously optimistic that someone's putting effort into your wife's murder. It wasn't about her. It wasn't about the kids. Your first reaction was whether you were going to be charged. If you think in your heart of hearts this "I don't know, wasn't there" is going to work, then why would you worry about being charged? Has anyone ever said that to you?

One has to wonder what Greg thought after this interview. One thing is for sure, he knew the police still hadn't given up after all these years which had to have surprised him. But still, Greg was a true sociopath. I am sure he thought he had nothing to worry about.

TWELVE

In the Spring of 2016 everything changed.

One day, Julie told me that Dana called her because they wanted DNA samples from the boys. I was stunned.

We didn't know that the Illinois State Police and the Piatt County States Attorney's office had been working the case, at least in any serious way. I had pretty much come to terms with the fact that Greg was never going to face justice for killing Sheryl.

Dana seemed to think they might have enough to charge Greg with murder but there was a serious issue to overcome. They had done more DNA tests on Sheryl's nightgown and found bloodspots that didn't match Greg's. If it wasn't Greg's blood on the nightgown, that would pretty much be the definition of reasonable doubt. Investigators wanted to test the boys' blood, as one of them could have been hurt in some manner and got blood on the nightgown.

My emotions were all over the place. I was extremely excited because after all of these years Dana and the police seemed to be closing in on Greg. But still, doubt crept in.

I dreaded telling my parents and the boys. If Dana needed DNA from them, someone was going to have to tell them why—their dad was being investigated for the murder of their mother. This would be the definition of saying the quiet part out loud. None of us had ever breathed a word of this to them.

I wanted to tell my parents immediately. I didn't want anyone telling them before I got to them first. I talked to Julie and Lisa and they were hesitant to tell Mom and dad and get their hopes up once again. They weren't even sure if Mom and Dad would want to pursue it now after all these years.

They didn't seem to understand that it wasn't our choice. An act such as murder is a crime against the State and the State has the ultimate decision as to whether to file charges and pursue a conviction or not. I hadn't talked to Dana or anyone else of authority at this point, but I knew if they wanted DNA from the boys, they were serious about pursuing charges.

I always wondered if my mother would live to see justice for Sheryl. I had started to doubt it.

In November of 2014, my mother had open heart surgery. It was a little touch and go for a bit but she made it through and was starting to get stronger again.

Lisa, Julie, and I agreed to say something to my mom and dad, but we decided to make it as casual as we could. We wanted them to be aware there was activity, but we didn't want to give them false hopes. It didn't seem right to withhold information from them. My mom was excited but nervous about what it all meant. My dad was lukewarm on the idea. He was concerned about the boys and how they would take it. I explained the situation to my parents like I had to my sisters—we don't have control over this.

I was a little annoyed. This moment was something we had all yearned for all these years and now that it looked like it was going to happen, some were having second thoughts. This was understandable. Life had gone on and there were a lot of lives that were going to be adversely affected by the case being reopened. However, just because it might make some people uncomfortable doesn't mean you should just let someone get away with murder. Greg killed my sister.

I didn't care if his arrest and conviction made anyone feel awkward.

We were going to have to talk to the boys. There were no two ways around it. It wasn't as if they weren't going to find out. There was no protecting them any longer from the fact their father was a murderer. I could tell from the look in my mother's eyes that it was all on me again. I could hear her in my mind, "You started this, Renee. Now you need to finish it. Take care of it. Get justice for Sheryl and while you're at it, don't hurt the boys." I had to comply and I knew I couldn't disappoint her this time. The pressure was almost unbearable.

The boys had no idea any of this was even happening. I am still not sure and I will probably never be sure if they knew Greg killed their mother, but they definitely didn't know he was being investigated. To them, it was all over and no one was thinking about it anymore. Julie, Lisa, and I agreed that I should call each of them and let them know that we had just been advised the Piatt County States Attorney and the Illinois State Police were looking into their mother's death.

When I made the calls, I was to tell each of them their mother did not commit suicide. That was clear even way back then. We knew she had been murdered and we suspected their father but he had never been arrested. We had just been advised that the case is being worked and was progressing without our knowledge. This was not about anything that I had done recently.

This was important to me. I loved them and had worked hard to protect them all these years. I didn't want to hurt them now and I certainly didn't want them to be mad at me or my sisters or blame me or any of us for their father being prosecuted for their mother's murder.

I called the oldest first. He looked out for his two brothers so he needed to know initially because I knew the other two would call him for his opinion and advice as soon as they received the news.

I explained the same thing to each of them that I had to my parents. None of them really had much of a reaction. I wasn't surprised. How could they have not suspected this would happen some day?

I told them that the State wanted their DNA. I carefully explained to them that it was not for the purpose of attempting to prove that any of them had anything to do with their mother's death. I didn't want to give too much information away so I explained investigators had found blood at the scene, that they didn't know whose it was, and they wanted to see if it was possibly theirs. It was their house, and they were young after all. All sorts of things happened at that age that could cause bleeding.

Each of them could provide a swab of the inside of their mouths voluntarily or the State would issue a subpoena and get it that way. I gave them the number to call to arrange to have it done and told them that it could all be very discreet.

The conversation with the oldest was smooth but more than a little heart wrenching. I knew it would be. He has Sheryl's sweet and sensitive heart and soul and I could tell this made him very uncomfortable. It was obvious he had blocked so much of this tragedy out and he had no interest in dredging it back up.

When I asked him if he would cooperate, he said, "I guess" and sounded noncommittal, but I repeated to him they could subpoena him. He said nothing which wasn't a surprise as he internalizes everything. He agreed to do it but it took him awhile and a few follow-up phone calls from me telling him, "If you don't reach out, you will get a subpoena and I don't want that stress for you." He provided the sample shortly thereafter.

The conversation with the youngest was easy. He was only 18 months old when it happened and had never really bonded with Greg. My parents in essence were the only parents he had ever known. He was fascinated with what was going on almost as if he was a stranger being told about the case. He was just like "Oh cool, Aunt Renee, no problem." It didn't seem to faze him even a little bit. I knew he would cooperate. He called right away and got it taken care of.

I called the middle boy last. I knew he would be the most confrontational about the news. I told him the case was being investigated. He asked me why I was doing this after all these years. I told him I wasn't doing anything. Investigators called me and I was going to cooperate. It was something the whole family wanted. He said he lived in Georgia and they can't get to him and he wasn't going to do it. I told him they could get a subpoena and they would if they had to. He said he was going to hire an attorney and fight it. He wouldn't listen to me. He hired an attorney in Georgia and decided to resist providing a sample. Ultimately, just like I had explained, a subpoena was issued, transferred to Georgia, and Georgia police went to his home and obtained his sample.

After this, the investigation really picked up steam. I knew that there was no stopping now. We had a State's Attorney and committed Illinois State Police detectives who had never given up hope. It was obvious to me that they had the case close to where they needed it to be before they filed charges. I was thrilled that someone was finally committed to obtaining a conviction. I did whatever they needed me to do to help.

I went to my basement and dug out two plastic tubs that I had moved six times from Florida to my current home. I didn't know if I would ever need these documents, but I couldn't bear to ever part with them. They contained all my notes, correspondence, and court pleadings from the last 26 years. When I started looking through the files, tears flowed and all the old memories flooded back. I closed the lid on the boxes and called Dana and told her what I had. She came that day to my house and picked up my boxes. She thanked me, saying they would be helpful. She could sense my reluctance to turn my files over but she assured me that they would take it from here.

Standing on my driveway that warm spring day with the sun shining on my face and watching Dana drive away with those boxes, I looked to the sky and told Sheryl, "I think we are really going to find justice for you in our lifetime, in Mom's lifetime."

I'm a woman of faith and I told myself many times over the years, that even if we didn't see it, he would someday pay. The ultimate judgment day doesn't escape any of us.

Now that I knew this was really happening and others were in charge, I needed to focus on my mom and dad and the boys. My mom's excitement continued to grow. All of us started to come to grips with the reality that this was really happening. So many feelings raced through me. I was excited, of course, but I was terrified that he would be tried and not convicted and then where would we be? Could my parents survive that? I was sick to my stomach thinking about the impact on the boys.

Dana talked to me and my sisters about whether we were prepared to try the case and lose, and the effect it would have on our family. Could my parents actually withstand the trial, sit there and listen to all of this and watch Sheryl get dragged through the mud by Greg's defense? I was ready for anything. If nothing else, the story would be told and people would know what really happened. But if my parents weren't ready to go through this and live with a jury's decision, we couldn't do it. But then again, we didn't have the ultimate say. The State got to make that decision, not us.

My mom was adamant that she could handle the stress. She was finally going to see her daughter's murderer held accountable. She had been praying and waiting 26 years for this day.

Dana' assistant, Elizabeth Dobson, researched the use of a psychological autopsy and located an expert in Champaign,

Illinois who had experience with these. A psychological autopsy is used to identify the state of mind of a person before their death. Dana and Elizabeth were intrigued with the idea. It might be just what they needed to rebut what they knew would be a key defense, which was Sheryl had committed suicide. I researched the concept and use of such reports in criminal cases and the doctor they discovered who was to do this for them—Dr. Lawrence Jeckel. My research indicated that such reports had been used for years in courts, in other high profiles cases. I was impressed with Dana and Elizabeth's thoroughness and desire to push the envelope and be cutting edge.

Dana and Elizabeth planned to convene another coroner's jury and conduct a second inquest. Initially, I wondered why; it made no sense to me. Later, I realized it was absolutely ingenious. As before, the coroner's inquest had no legal significance to a criminal matter. It was a bit of an archaic process still on the books in Illinois that allowed a coroner to convene a jury to determine cause of death for a death certificate. Sheryl's had previously been decided to be "undetermined". That had always bothered us, but it was never a top concern. However, Dana and Elizabeth concluded they had the right to convene a second coroner's jury and change the cause of death on Sheryl's death certificate.

This could prove beneficial to them in several ways. The State would be able to conduct a mini trial with the current evidence and in essence have a dry run or practice trial before they proceeded with murder charges and a murder trial. They would be able to call witnesses and elicit testimony again from key witnesses such as Greg, Les Shores, and Tim Byrd. It would be interesting to see if they could repeat their same stories after all these years or perhaps even break and tell secrets we all suspected they had been holding. And perhaps the most significant thing to me was if nothing else ever happened, my parents could have the satisfaction of having

Sheryl's death certificate accurately reflect what we all knew the cause of death to be—homicide.

On July 8, 2016, a second inquest was held. A jury was convened, witnesses were called, Greg was called although he did nothing but plead his fifth amendment rights. I testified. A few law enforcement folks were called. The jury deliberated and quickly ruled that the cause of death was homicide. It felt like the tide was turning. The Illinois State Police began another round of interviews trying to stir things up and put the pressure on a few key people.

I told the boys they could call and ask me anything and I would tell them honestly what I knew about the case. I tried my best to keep them apprised of the major events happening.

One night, the middle boy called me and said, "Call them off." I said I didn't know what he was talking about. He said, "You call them off. They're going to interview Grandpa." At first, I thought he was talking about my dad. It took me a minute to realize that he was talking about Grandpa Houser. Once I realized who he meant, I told him I wasn't in charge, and regardless, he shouldn't be angry with me, he should be angry with Greg. I didn't do any of this. I didn't kill anyone.

He was playing the victim. He was too young to remember the pain we all suffered and he didn't want to experience any of it himself now. He said to me that even if Greg killed Sheryl, what good would it do after all these years to convict him now? I couldn't even respond to that. It was obvious he wasn't being rational and he wanted to avoid confrontation and pain. While I certainly understood where he was coming from, I don't believe in allowing a murderer to get away with his crime just because he had gotten away with it for years and it would cause emotional pain to people to bring it up now. I was very much of the opinion that the only way a person could fight their internal demons was to face them head on. I hoped and prayed he and the other boys might do that someday for their own mental health.

Near the end of July, 2016, Elizabeth indicated she had information from Dr. Jeckel that she wanted to share with us. Elizabeth told us that Walt Rohr, Sheryl's friend who Greg was so jealous of, contacted them via his attorney after they requested a recent DNA sample from him. Evidently, he didn't entirely understand DNA and he wanted to now confess, although he had denied it at the time of Sheryl's death and again in 2015 when he was reinterviewed, that he and Sheryl had one sexual encounter. Elizabeth wanted us to hear this news from her because we had all been so adamant that Sheryl had never had an affair.

While I was a bit surprised by the actions of my straight-laced sister, I was happy for her. Perhaps the sexual experience she had with Walt was tender and caring and not forced, demanded, or plain rape like she so often experienced with her husband. Elizabeth also told us that Dr. Jeckel would like to meet with all of us.

Elizabeth wrote that they were preparing to file first degree murder charges against Greg as soon as the next day. Once charges were filed, they would ask the judge for an arrest warrant, bond would be set, and the trial would start by October, 2016. She warned us to anticipate another round of media coverage.

After all these years, it was go time. This was really going to happen. Excitement, terror, panic, and relief all flooded in at once. It was hard to breathe let alone try and reconcile all the different feelings surging through my body.

It turned out to be a false alarm. Later that same day, Elizabeth called and said that charges would be delayed. There were a few critical leads being tracked down and a couple more interviews in the works which they wanted to complete. Dr. Jeckel had not rendered his final report and it would be good to have that before charges were actually filed. I told her that we had all waited 26 years for this, a few more weeks won't make a difference.

On September 22, 2016, my sisters and I received the following e-mail from Elizabeth: "Ladies: I am sorry to be cryptic about this – I hope you will understand that there are officer safety issues to consider, so Dana and I cannot provide information until the police work is accomplished. Today is the day that the case will start, so you may want to be prepared for media attention to the case, certainly by tomorrow."

I could barely breathe as I read the email. I called Julie and Lisa. It was clear murder charges would be filed and Greg would be arrested. We planned to stay in contact and not say anything to Mom until we got word from Elizabeth that Greg was in custody.

The anticipation was killing me. I had to do something. I went outside and started working in the yard, which was always good therapy for me. I began to mow the lawn. I didn't want to miss the call so I tucked my phone in my bra. I knew if I didn't hear the ring, I would at least feel the vibration.

After a few moments on the riding lawnmower, I felt my phone vibrating against my heart. I killed the engine on the mower and struggled to get my phone out of my shirt. It was Lisa. I excitedly answered with a quick hello. Lisa said he had been arrested. I couldn't believe it. After all these years, he was going to pay.

I called Julie as Lisa ran over to my mom's. We wanted to be the ones to tell her. We didn't want it to be like the day Sheryl was found and she and my dad heard about it through the grapevine. It was too late as Greg had already been arrested at a gas station. A friend of my mom's was there when Greg was arrested and called my mother immediately.

The cops had waited at a gas station and convenience store in Mansfield where he stopped after work every day to buy beer. When he came out, they tackled him to the ground, handcuffed his hands behind his back, and arrested him. He had no idea it was about to happen; he was too damn cocky. Some people in the community knew, but no one told him. Before he could even be taken away to jail, his mom and dad arrived on the scene demanding to know what was happening and saying how unfair it was. If his attorney, Keith Hayes, had still been alive, I'm sure he would have been there too. His parents were on their own this time.

As I pulled into my parents' driveway, the middle boy and his girlfriend pulled in next to me. I said to Travis, "Hey Travis! I want to let you know something."

He got out of the car and said, "I already know."

I said, "How do you know?" and he said, "Because Gramma is in the house talking and laughing on the phone about it with her friends and you need to tell her to stop talking about it in the house because I don't want to hear it."

I lost it.

I said, "That is Gramma's house. Sheryl, your mother, is her daughter. Your dad murdered her daughter. She can talk about him being arrested in her house if she wants to and if you don't want to hear it, get your sorry ass out."

He said, "You're going to have to get the cops to get me out of here because I am not leaving."

I replied, "Are you really standing here telling me Gramma can't make you leave? Don't tempt me because I will get the cops out here and you will be removed."

As began to leave I yelled at him, "Your fucking dad murdered my sister! He is guilty and I am glad he is going to jail where he belongs!"

He got in the car and sped away and I went in the house shaking. I told my parents what happened. My mom said he would get over it and he was just upset.

I felt terrible. I never intended to exchange such angry words with him. My heart went out to him. He didn't choose his father and he didn't have anything to do with his father killing his mother. He was just an innocent child and no child wants a bad father.

I couldn't deal with it when he demanded my mother not be excited and stop talking about it. After all, it was her daughter and she had waited 26 years for this day. It was an exciting day and we wanted to celebrate.

But once again, we had to hide our emotions. We had protected them for years by not talking about it at our own emotional expense and here we were feeling like we needed to protect them again, not being allowed to talk about his arrest or show our excitement. I didn't think I could do that again. They were not boys anymore; they were grown men. As hard as I knew it was going to be, I was glad that perhaps with the secret out they could all face the demons I know haunted them all at times, love themselves for who they had become, and move on with their lives without the burden of the unspoken secret we kept from them.

THIRTEEN

Twenty-six years.

Greg had walked free for 26 years and it finally happened. He had been arrested. But we still weren't out of the woods yet. We needed a conviction. We also needed to keep our family together, and that wasn't going to be easy.

After the confrontation with Travis, I called the other two boys to check on them. The youngest seemed fine as I suspected. The oldest was a mess. We had a gut-wrenching conversation in which both of us cried many tears. I was so emotional at one point I realized that I was driving 40 mph on the interstate during our conversation. I couldn't think straight. I wanted to fix everything for him. I wanted to take away his pain. I wanted to erase the picture that he told me he couldn't get out of his mind. It was so unfair. They were just babies. If Greg had been arrested and convicted back then, they could have had 26 years of healing behind them. Now the healing process was just beginning for them and, in reality, for all of us.

Greg's arraignment was set for the following Monday. I wanted to attend. We all did. We wanted to see Greg in police custody, in a jail uniform with his hands behind his back. We had all waited a long time for that day. Dana and Elizabeth agreed that doing so for many victims can be the start of a long healing process.

I thought I was prepared to see him up close and in person, which I hadn't done in years. His appearance was shocking to me. I don't know that if I had seen him on the street, I would have immediately recognized him. Time and guilt had not served him well. He was pale, overweight, unshaven, and generally unkempt. I thought seeing him this time, this way, would be different than when I had encountered him in the past but it wasn't. The sight of him took my breath away. It is hard to look at a person and know that they personally choked the life out of your loved one. I can't even begin to understand how one human can do that to another. Rage set in. I wanted to jump over the banister in the courtroom separating the audience from the proceedings and demand that he look at me. He kept his head down. His chin was nearly glued to his chest. He wouldn't look at anyone.

The judge didn't address bond at his arraignment. A familiar feeling flooded back. We were terrified of him and worried about the boys. I testified during the bond hearing that he could kill someone to keep from going to jail which is what he did in the first place. I pleaded with the judge not to fail our family again. The following is my statement to him:

> *It's not just fear my family and I anticipate if he is released - it's terror.*

> *Last time Greg was out on bond he was pissed - he wasn't in control, he wasn't winning and it looked like people might hear Sheryl's story and he might have to suffer consequences for his treatment of her. It's my opinion that he solved that problem by killing her - the main witness in the case pending against him.*

His plan worked. For the last 26 years he has been in total control again. She is dead and her story couldn't be told. He and his family have always contended that she committed suicide. Life's been good. His problems went away, he has been free to do whatever he wanted.

Now, he perceives the family is doing this to him and I bet he is pissed - he isn't in control and he may not be free to do whatever he wants.

-

People don't understand the legal process. Because I am an attorney, they think I've been pursuing this and finally got him arrested. Even his family believes this. Through one of Sheryl's children, John Houser demanded that we make this stop.

Despite being free to do whatever he wanted, he didn't choose to forge a father-son relationship with his boys or voluntarily support them emotionally or financially.

Then 26 years later, after it was obvious to him a serious investigation was taking place in Sheryl's murder, he showed up at a son's house with a baby gift and wants to be a part of their life? He's not that nice and it's a little late to be that easy. He showed up to intimidate them because he wanted "it" to stop.

If he killed Sheryl to "win", to stay in control, I fear he could do it again. It worked once. Why wouldn't it work again? The thing that leads me to say it's not fear that this caused for me and my family but terror- is because none of us know who he thinks is responsible for challenging him this time (last time it was clearly Sheryl). This time is it me, my parents, the boys, her friends, the investigators, the State's attorney? Will he go after any of us or all of us? Based on past behavior, it's not unreasonable to think he will try again what worked for him last time.

Unfortunately, I believe the justice system failed my sister, her boys, and my family 26 years ago. I certainly hope they don't fail us again.

Please don't let him out. It's bad enough that all of us not only have to live through this horrific story again, I certainly hope we don't have to live through it while also being in fear for our safety.

Thankfully, the judge denied bail.

Dana rehired Rod Englert as an expert witness. He and his team of investigators received permission to go to the crime scene so they could restage it. The owner of the home had no idea there had ever been a murder in his home. The house looked exactly the same, it even had the same old carpet.

Rod was prepared to testify at trial as to the cause of death being manual strangulation. Perhaps more importantly, he was going to testify as to the source of the blood on Sheryl's nightgown being from morgue contamination. In his opinion, the angle of the drops of blood on her nightgown were not consistent with those being deposited on her nightgown at the scene.

At a pretrial conference in November of 2016, the defense asked for a continuance of the trial saying they needed more time to prepare. The law guaranteed the right to a speedy trial so the case needed to be brought to trial within 120 days of being taken into custody unless the delay is requested by the defendant. Because they requested the delay, the trial was continued. We weren't disappointed. We were still waiting on a final report from Dr. Jeckel and DNA evidence regarding the blood stains on her nightgown. To my family, this meant that we could go through the holidays without a January trial date weighing on us.

Dr. Jeckel completed his final report. Although countless people's DNA, including numerous members of my family, were compared for a match, none could be found.

The trial was set for April 3rd. That date came and went as the defense contended they still weren't ready. It didn't appear that the defense was going to hire any experts of their own. They had now filed their answer to the charges and were claiming two affirmative defenses: which were that Greg had an alibi; and self-defense, which meant if he was there and killed Sheryl, he did it in self-defense. This seemed ludicrous to me but at this point in this case, nothing much surprised me. The trial was set for July of 2017.

I corresponded with Elizabeth regularly about preparations for trial. I wanted to be aware of everything and help where I could. I was very worried about witnesses, their preparation, and how they would handle the stress of it all. In particular, I was worried about my parents and the boys. In May, I expressed these concerns in an e-mail to Elizabeth. She replied to me, "You have carried the burden of this whole situation for a long time, Renee. Not only what happened to your sister, but investigating the whole case, and then being the rock for your family. I know you can handle this, but if I were to tell the truth, I would say I worry about you more than I do about your parents. …You have to try to think of yourself as a victim here, too, and cut yourself some slack."

This made me sob. Elizabeth is perhaps the only person to see through my authoritativeness and businesslike approach to the case. She gave me permission for the first time in 26 years to be a victim.

By mid-June, we had Rod Englert, Dr. Denton, and Jennifer Aper lined up as expert witnesses. All shared the opinion that the unexplained blood drops on Sheryl's nightgown were from morgue contamination. Aper worked for the Illinois Crime Lab and was to testify as to how different the protocols were when the case was new and how this very easily could have happened.

We were relieved to have an explanation when it came to the unidentified blood. In my mind, this was the only thing the defense could possibly argue that a jury might consider as reasonable doubt. They could say the blood was from the real killer who was still out there. This was not necessarily reasonable in my mind but when it came to this case, my mind wasn't always rational.

The week before the trial, Dana and Elizabeth asked us to come in and observe photos that would be shown at trial. They wanted us to prepare ourselves by seeing them so whatever emotional reaction we might have initially would not be in public.

This helped each of us determine whether we could sit through that part of the trial. My parents decided they would leave the courtroom when the photos were shown. They didn't want to see crime scene and autopsy photos. My sisters and I broke down when we looked at the photos. I had worked on this case all these years and had these very photos in my possession but never had the guts or desire to look at them. The tears and the anger came back as if it were October 25, 1990. I was thankful for the opportunity to grieve in private. During this part of the trial, I decided I would not look at the photos, rather I would stare at Greg and watch his reaction.

It wouldn't be easy for my mother to hear what was going to be said in the courtroom. True or not, one never wants to hear the kinds of things said about their daughter that she was going to hear. During the trial, a lot of it was too much for my father so he ended up leaving the room.

Going into the trial, I was a bit worried about Judge Koritz. He was young and didn't have a lot of murder trial experience. When the trial began, I didn't know what to think. He had a constant poker face and seemed to rule in the defense' favor more often than not. But he was thoughtful and methodical and I could tell he had done his research and was well prepared so I reserved judgment.

The trial was set to begin on Monday, July 3, 2017. Jury selection started July 3. Greg was brought to the courtroom looking vastly different then when I last saw him. His hair was neatly cut, his face clean shaven, and he had ditched his orange jumpsuit and flip flops for dress slacks, a shirt and tie, and dress shoes. He was allowed to sit freely at the defense table.

We went to court every day as a family. We were all unified. My friend, Ann-Margret, came from Florida to join my family at the trial. We all wore purple ribbons in support of Sheryl. The courtroom was small and the seating was reminiscent of church pews. We sat in the front row behind the prosecution table. On the other side, his mom and dad sat with an aunt of Greg's. Everyone else in the room was a supporter of Sheryl.

There were lots of media there right from the start. There were pretrial hearings on what types of cameras would be allowed and what they could film. Huey Freeman from the *Piatt County Journal* wrote about the story when Sheryl was killed. All these years later, he covered the whole trial. I made a few public statements against Elizabeth's advice. In my opinion, if the media doesn't hear from you, they tell their own stories.

From the first moment Greg walked into the courtroom, he was so arrogant and pompous. It just oozed off of him. Did he convince himself he didn't do it? Or was he just a sociopath? He just sat there smirking and looked smug. I wanted to go up and punch him. Was he proud of himself and his work? Of how he eluded all of us for so long? He left a condom on the ground and the rope around her neck, the result of his despicable act looked nothing like an actually hanging. He did a bunch of dumb things, but he got away with it for a long time.

He said he loved her and still wanted to be with her but after she "committed suicide" he never had any sort of emotional reaction about the crime. During the trial, he rarely talked to his attorneys but would occasionally write furiously on a pad of paper. I knew him well enough to know he was seething inside.

Adding to the bizarre scene was the fact that Curtis Lovelace was in attendance at the trial. Lovelace was a football star at the University of Illinois, who was arrested for the murder of his wife, Cory.

He was charged with smothering his wife with a pillow the night before Valentine's Day in 2006 in their bed while their four young children slept in adjacent rooms. His defense was she died of natural causes related to her alcoholism, exacerbated by bulimia, which she also suffered from.

It was a high-profile crime. He was eventually found not guilty and was convinced for some bizarre reason, that Greg was not guilty as well. He showed up every day, grandstanding and making a spectacle of himself.

The jury was selected and on July 6, 2017, the trial began. Dana opened up and explained the process. She talked of how defense was going to say Greg didn't commit the crime and how there was only circumstantial evidence but hammered home the fact that DNA found in the condom proved he killed Sheryl.

The defense opened with Greg's attorney, Kevin Sanborn of the Johnson Law Group, arguing the State was woefully short of proving Greg guilty beyond a reasonable doubt. They mentioned Greg was the one who filed for divorce, that Sheryl had an affair, and that the state was completely lacking in evidence. I wasn't impressed with

Sanborn throughout the trial and felt that Greg was seriously underrepresented. Not that I was upset by that mind you.

The first witness Dana called was Sheryl. A young female attorney from Monticello read her prior testimony in from Greg's assault trial. It was incredibly powerful.

Then other witnesses came, all of them presenting damning evidence against Greg.

Tim Byrd testified that Sheryl was a close friend of his. He said he was only vaguely aware of their divorce which strained credibility. He admitted watching her in the cornfield with Les and Greg to see if she was having an affair. He claimed he had very little memory of who was at the party that fateful night.

Rod Englert testified about his reconstruction of the murder scene. He was a great witness who detailed how the rope around Sheryl's neck was too tight for suicide and made many other damning points that had the defense on the defensive.

The next day I was the first witness of day. I really wanted to testify at the trial for so many reasons. I had prepared so many people for trial. I knew how to listen, answer questions, and otherwise behave on the stand. I had proven I was effective as a witness at the 2nd inquest and the bond hearing. The court setting didn't intimidate me and Greg's attorneys certainly did not intimidate me. In my mind, it was a chance to complete my act of helping my beloved sister, 27 years after I began.

Before my testimony, I met with Dana, Elizabeth, and Roger to prepare. They asked Roger to be there because he and I together had so much history we would be able to refresh each other's memories on details. It was comforting as we had formed a relationship over the years and, while we hadn't stayed in contact, the connection was still there.

They went through the standard witness preparation litany and then got into what they needed from me. They wanted me to give the background on Sheryl's journal she had been keeping and authenticate the actual journals because I recognized her handwriting. They also wanted me to talk about Sheryl and the kind of person she was, her love for the boys, her plans for the future, and my opinion based on all that that she did not commit suicide. I was ready to defend Sheryl. I was ready to be her voice that had been silenced for so many years.

When my name was called and I raised my hand to be sworn in, I had a moment when I wasn't sure if this experience was real or a dream. Dana quickly put me at ease with her demeanor and simple opening questions. I was emotional. That surprised me a bit but I could not stop the tears from seeping slowly out of my eyes. I knew it was ok though. It made me more real to the jury. I looked and spoke directly to the jurors. I tried to look at different ones at different times but I didn't want to look at anyone for too long. I didn't want to make them uncomfortable. The ones who made eye contact with me relaxed me. I could see the sympathy in their eyes for me, my family, the boys, and for Sheryl.

Sanborn didn't cross examine me; his partner did. It didn't matter. I was ready. When you are honest and passionate, yet controlled, it's easy to tell your story and answer questions. He tried to be tough with me. I remained calm but firm in my responses. I wasn't about to let him twist anything I said. My strategy worked and his approach backfired. I am sure the jury didn't appreciate him trying to be tough with me. At this moment in time, I was truly a victim and Dana and Elizabeth had given me the permission to be just that. I'll be forever grateful to them for that. It helped my testimony, but more importantly, it helped me start a healing process that I didn't even realized at the time never got underway. Once I was done testifying, a big burden was lifted. I truly had done everything in my power to help Sheryl.

I was followed by Mom, Dad, and the oldest boy. My father's testimony was hard to sit through. He cried on the stand, and I could tell he blamed himself, saying things such as, "if only I had stayed; if only she had taken the gun from me."

That same day Elizabeth wrote to me in an email, "Win or lose, I hope that you will all know that you have done everything possible to represent Sheryl and the love that you all have for her is remarkable."

On July 10, Deputy McCabe testified he was dispatched to Sheryl and Greg's house on August 8, 1990. When he got there, Greg was outside and he could smell alcohol on his breath. He arrested Greg for battery and took him to jail. Then on September 20, 1990, he went to Chris and Jackie's house for a 911 call. Sheryl was there crying. She had red marks on her neck and abrasions on both sides of her mouth and one near her eye. There were blood stains on the sheets by her pillowcase consistent with rope across her mouth.

Alan Hardy testified. He worked with Greg and went to school with him. Greg told him he found her journals and made copies and took them to his attorney trying to prove she was an unfit mother. One day, Alan told him at work, "You look awful." Greg said, "You would too if you had been sitting in a cornfield watching your house."

Julie Roth, who was on of Sheryl's best friends since high school, said on the stand that Sheryl was upbeat and planning for the future and there was no way she committed suicide.

Next came Chris Doenitz who told of opening the door on September 20th and Sheryl falling into his arms crying and frantic. He then called the sheriff. He also testified about the day of the murder where he arrived at the house the same time as Greg. Chris testified Greg was not visibly upset at the scene of Sheryl's murder.

Deputy Dunlap testified as to seeing Les driving near Greg's grandparents' house the night of the murder, first alone, then with another person in the car. Greg seemed a bit nervous during this, writing notes and whispering to his attorney with his hand over his mouth.

.

Philip Sallee and Jennifer Aper, both forensic scientists for the Illinois State Police, testified about DNA testing back then and how it has progressed. When the murder occurred, the DNA testing wasn't very exact. When they tested the fluid, they couldn't say it was Greg's DNA for sure. All they could say is that he could not be excluded. When they retested with the advancements in DNA, they concluded it was her DNA on the outside of the condom and his on the inside.

Dr. Denton, a forensic pathologist, educated the jury on bruises, broken capillaries, and strangulation death. He testified the death was a homicide and the blood on the nightgown is due to cross contamination.

Another witness, Kevin Phelps, who worked at Southland with Greg, testified that one day while in the break room talking with Greg he said he would use a rope and do what he did to her what he did with his deer.

There were more witnesses as well, all of whom testified to what I already knew. Greg killed Sheryl.

At 9:45, the State rested early in an attempt to catch the defense off guard. Greg's attorney then moved for a directed verdict which is a motion that contends that there is not enough evidence at the close of the state's case to even present the case to the jury. Judge Koritz denied this motion.

The defense didn't have a lot to counter with. One notable witness was Walt Rohr who admitted he had sex once with Sheryl in a hotel room.

As we suspected, Greg did not testify. The defense rested at 2:10.

The next day, during closing arguments, Dana spoke to how circumstantial evidence gave rise to a reasonable inference and a logical conclusion that Greg is, in fact, guilty. She made clear though her words there was no way this was a suicide. It was staged. The bruises on her neck, the loops in the rope, the tip of the glove, and DNA testing all were consistent with manual strangulation. She then walked the jury through Greg's prior criminal acts, and the orders of protection.

"The person knew the scene, knew the layout, knew what materials that (sic) would be available so that they could stage this hanging suicide to cover up their tracks for strangling Sheryl Houser," she said. "The defense wants you to believe this is a stunning set of coincidences that are just not credible in this case."

As always, Dana did an incredible job. She was calm, collected, and laser focused on the facts.

When the defense had their turn, they repeated there was no evidence and that Greg had an alibi. Even though the fact was there was a lot of evidence and Greg's alibi was awful. They also tried to blame things on Walt Rohr of all people.

"This case is rife with reasonable doubt," Sanborn said, and added that the net of potential suspects should have been widened to include Walt Rohr. Sanborn pointed out that Rohr lied to investigators at least twice about his relationship with Sheryl.

"This known liar, someone who lied during a homicide investigation, is apparently walking free. He was never arrested or charged with lying to police, providing false information during a homicide investigation," Sanborn continued.

Trying to blame the murder on Walt Rohr? The whole defense seemed incredibly weak to me, but at the same point I was biased as Sheryl was my sister. Who knew what these jurors would do?

The judge instructed the jury to consider all evidence, including circumstantial. At 1:00 p.m., the jury went to deliberate.

And that was that. After all of these years, it was in the hands of the jury.

Each day at lunch we went as a family to the house of good friends of Julie's. They had been so kind to open their home to us as a place to go and relax away from everything.

When the jury retired to the jury room for deliberations, my family went to our friends' house as usual. I couldn't go. I didn't want to be with anyone and I didn't want to leave the courthouse. I was so keyed up and nervous. I honestly didn't know what the outcome would be; I couldn't imagine being around people and having lunch.

Joe talked me into walking to a local restaurant and splitting a sandwich with him but I ate quickly and insisted that we go right back to the courthouse. I wanted to sit in Dana's office until I was notified the jury was back. Dana and Elizabeth went to lunch and were taking care of other business. So I sat there by myself staring into space and waiting. My stomach was in knots.

Finally, at 3:33 my phone buzzed with a text message. The jury reached a verdict. I waited outside the courtroom for my family. When they arrived, we filed back in the courtroom and took our seats.

They came back in under two hours. It took 27 years for him to be brought to trial and the jury decided in under two hours.

We all stood together holding hands. I had my head down and my eyes closed. We had previously agreed that no matter what happened there would be no emotional outbursts, one way or the other. No yelling or screaming or making spectacles of ourselves.

The judge took the bench at 3:51 and asked the foreman if the jury had reached a verdict to which the foreman replied "Yes." The written verdict was passed from the foreman to the judge via the bailiff. The judge announced that the jury found the defendant, Gregory Houser, guilty of first degree murder of Sheryl Houser.

It was surreal. For a moment I thought I might be dreaming. Then the tears came. I didn't know if they were tears of joy or relief or sadness but it didn't really matter. We had obtained justice for Sheryl and my parents were alive to see it happen.

When Dana turned around, I saw she was crying too. We embraced.

Greg was immediately taken out of court. He had no reaction to the charges. His parents slid by us and out of the courtroom.

Dana and Elizabeth ushered us into a back room to celebrate a bit more in private and wait for the crowd to leave. We hoped to stay long enough for the reporters to leave, too, but they waited us out. I read a prepared statement thanking everyone for their hard work in finally obtaining justice for Sheryl.

Before I left, I saw Greg brought out of the courtroom. His head was pushed down as he was put into the van taking him to prison, hopefully for the rest of his life. It was an indescribable feeling seeing him get his last taste of freedom.

We all gathered back at our friends in Monticello for a private celebration. Even at this moment, we were mindful of the boys and their feelings and wanted to make sure our emotions were expressed first outside their presence. But make no mistake about it, that celebration was full of joy and of satisfaction. Sheryl had finally received justice

FOURTEEN

While Greg being convicted of murder didn't bring Sheryl back, nothing ever could after all, we had won. He was going to prison.

He would be appropriately punished. I wasn't worried about that at all. Dana and Elizabeth explained long ago that if they obtained a conviction, he would be sentenced under the laws that existed at the time of the crime. Thus, we knew the death penalty was off the table and we knew the maximum length of time he could be sentenced to was shorter than the current laws would have permitted. Still, I knew he was going away for a long time.

I wanted the conviction more than anything because I wanted to clear Sheryl's name and tell her story. It was time the world knew what a monster Greg Houser was and the torture he subjected Sheryl to on countless occasions. He was 58, overweight, a diabetic with rotten teeth, and addiction issues. He was also an abuser of women, antisocial, and a very prejudiced white male. I had no doubt he would not fare well in prison. In fact, the conditions he would be subjected to in prison made me smile when I thought about them. Karma is a bitch. He was going to get what he deserved.

On the other hand, my mom, while happy about the conviction, jumped right to expressing her worry that he would be lightly sentenced and would be out of prison in no time living life again. I didn't think I had the energy to go through it all again. I told her she needed to write an impact statement and express to the judge all her feelings about what Greg had caused and taken away from her and others. If she wanted the judge to give him the maximum sentence he was allowed by law, she needed to step up to the plate and tell him herself. I told her if she wrote it down, I would type it up and help get the statement in final form for her to read to the judge.

She did it. She wrote with passion and conviction and told the judge why he needed to be sentenced to the maximum years allowed. More importantly, my 80-year-old mother read her statement to the judge with an expression on her face that could only come from the heart of a mother whose daughter had had the life choked out of her by her abusive and controlling husband. At the end of her statement, she raised a photo of Sheryl in her nurse's uniform, a photo that portrayed just who Sheryl was. I was so proud of her. I felt bad for being angry with her for the stress I felt she placed on me. I was slowly starting to realize that no one caused my feelings but me.

I consulted with Julie and Lisa and we wrote a sisters' impact statement that Lisa read at sentencing on behalf of the three of us. Dana planned on using me as a witness. I would tell the judge of the impact Greg's actions caused me, my parents, sisters, the boys, their children, our extended family, and friends for the past 27 years and into the future emotionally, physically, financially then, now, and for generations to come.

I had spent the past 27 years preparing for this day. The words and tears both flowed easily. While the judge maintained the utmost professionalism, I looked him in the eyes and spoke directly through them to his heart. I could tell he heard us and understood us. I knew he was going to do the right thing.

Dana and Elizabeth brought Greg's prior girlfriends to the sentencing. While we had heard of other women in his life and abuse they suffered from him, it wasn't until they voluntarily appeared in court and shared their stories of abuse and terror did my heart go out to them. They didn't have to get involved. They didn't know us. But they came and they struggled through their own stories of abuse to help us lock up this monster and keep him from repeating the cycle of violence all over again; one that would cause more ripple effects for years to come.

When the judge rendered his ruling on the sentencing, I knew I had truly spoken to his heart. What follows are excerpts from his ruling[5]:

> *I'm torn with respect to whether I should go over the evidence that was presented at trial, and ultimately I decided that I will briefly touch upon that evidence because, one, Mr. Houser still asserts his innocence.*

> *Certainly, you have a right to do that, Mr. Houser. You have a right to certificate your innocence. You have a right to demand a trial. You have a right to be proven guilty beyond a reasonable doubt. Certainly, this Court would never hold that against you.*

> *And while the Court does not hold -- on one hand. the Court doesn't hold your maintenance of innocence against you on this at this time, the Court understands that there may be appeal to follow and that you are maintaining your innocence. But the Court does find as another statutory factor that you lack remorse. And Mr. Sanborn makes a good point, you lack remorse because you maintain your innocence. But I do find that as an aggravating*

---

5. This quote initially contained grammar, spelling and punctuation errors that have now been corrected for easier reading and comprehension.

factor because I do believe that there was sufficient evidence for the jury to consider in convicting you.

And I want to tell you why I do believe the jury had enough evidence to convict you.

Starting with the preliminary timeline, you and Sheryl were married. You had three small boys. Over the course of the marriage, the evidence shows that you were domineering and possibly physically abusive over the course of the marriage. The evidence shows that Sheryl put up with your domineering personality, or at least tended to tolerate it for some period of time, but that changed in the summer of 1990. The jury was entitled to accept the State's theme and premise that Sheryl grew more assertive during the summer of 1990.

On July 10th of 1990, you filed a Petition for Dissolution of Marriage. On July 19th, Sheryl filed a cross Petition for Dissolution of Marriage. On April -- I'm sorry, on August -- 9th, there was a battery report, police were called. The testimony was that you had held Sheryl down by the floor by her arms.

The arresting officer, or the reporting officer, saw bruising on Sheryl's upper arm. This is evidence that was presented at trial. And I'm not giving my opinion of the evidence, but I'm telling you why I believe the jury found sufficient evidence to convict you.

On August 28th of 1990, Sheryl petitioned for an Order of Protection. On that same day, she detailed a sexual assault report in her diary. The jury did not hear that report, did not hear that diary entry. But certainly the Court heard that here today. But the jury did hear that Sheryl did file an Order of Protection.

On September 4th,, Sheryl petitioned the Court for temporary custody. On September 12th an order was entered where you received half time with the kids, Sheryl received half time with the kids, and you each had -- the kids were nesting; in other words, you watched the kids in the house and you took turns in the house.

On September 20th, Sheryl reported a sexual assault. There was evidence presented at trial of that sexual assault. The jury was free to consider whether that actually happened. They were informed that they could only consider that for the purpose of motive, intent, and design.

On September 21, you were charged with criminal sexual assault by the Piatt County State's Attorney's Office. On September 24th, there was a hearing on Sheryl's petition for emergency relief based on, essentially, those allegations of sexual assault.

The September 12th order was revoked. Sheryl got the marital residence and full custody of the kids for the near future. And that was the context for what was to follow. That set the stage for the remainder of the State's evidence. And at that point, the jury was free to consider the State's premise and the State's theme that your personal life was crumbling, the marriage was on its way to dissolution, the marital residence was in the balance, custody of the children was in the balance. You had attempted to get your way by threats and force up to that time. Now facing charges of criminal sex assault you were looking at prison time as well as the likelihood that Sheryl would prevail on a number of issues in the dissolution proceeding, not the least of which were custody of the children and the marital residence.

You had previously demonstrated familiarity with the rope and the willingness to use the rope to inflict violence upon Sheryl, including strangulation or suffocation. And then on October 5th, Sheryl was discovered deceased.

The jury was free to consider was this a murder or a suicide, one; and if it was a murder, who did it, two. The jury could find that there was no credible evidence for suicide and, in fact, you conceded as much and your attorney conceded as much in closing arguments. The evidence, the jury found, strongly supported the notion that the murder was staged to appear like a suicide.

So then the jury could consider who did that, a stranger or someone known to Sheryl.

If it were to be a stranger, why was this house picked in the middle of a corn field?

There was no sign of a forced entry. How did the killer lure Sheryl outside of the house? And if the stranger killed Sheryl inside the house, how did he get in and how could it have been accomplished so quietly that the children were not disturbed and there was no sign of struggle inside?

The jury was free to consider what might a stranger's motive be. There was no obvious burglary or theft. The kids were unharmed and undisturbed. The jury was free to consider why would a stranger stage the scene to look like a suicide. That would take valuable time. What would the motive be to do that ? How would a stranger have familiarity with the garage, with the rope, with space in the rafter? That indicates planning and deliberate thought process. Why would a stranger -- would, would a stranger be less likely to be concerned with wearing rubber gloves during the offense?

But the jury was free to disregard the fact and find beyond a reasonable doubt that it was not a stranger that committed this crime. So then I imagine -- and I'm imagining -- the jury would turn to the fact that maybe it was somebody known to Sheryl. And the jury could consider that the evidence established that there was no motive for anybody in the world other than the Defendant, other than you, to kill Sheryl Houser. You had the opportunity, the motive and familiarity with the residence. You had the incentive to leave the children unharmed. You had no incentive to steal anything from the residence during the crime.

The crime was one of manual strangulation which suggests a very personal or emotional connection to the victim. You were the person who had been hiding in corn fields spying on Sheryl Houser previously that summer. You were the person who was heard to say earlier that summer that if Sheryl did not straighten up he would use the rope and do her like he did his deer.

It was your DNA found on a condom that was located feet from where Sheryl Houser remained suspended even though you stated you last had sexual contact with her on August 1st of 1990.

The jury was free to consider your actions the night before Sheryl Houser was found dead and the morning that she was found dead. The jury heard that you arrived on the scene, and witnesses recounted that they don't remember you having contact with your children on the scene. They don't recall you being very distraught at the scene.

You suggested to law enforcement that Sheryl Houser was depressed about finances, post-partum issues and Tim Byrd leaving. No other witness described Sheryl Houser in that manner. It's very consistent with somebody trying to convince law enforcement that the murder was a suicide which in turn was consistent with the motive of the killer in staging the homicide as a suicide.

Certainly the jury was free to consider that. The jury was free to consider your odd behavior the night before. You were seen at Tim Byrd's party. You left at 8 p.m. You went to your parents' house, where you were living, for 30 to 45 minutes.

Then, for some reason, you went to your grandparents to spend the night even though it was 9 p.m. around that time on a Thursday night even though it was the first time since being married to Sheryl Houser, in your words, that you spent the night at your grandparents. Why would you do that?

A jury could conclude that you were trying to create artificial alibi witnesses. A jury could reasonably infer that you knew your grandparents to be heavier sleepers than your parents and - and would not notice you gone during the night.

According to your interview, you woke up at 6:30 a.m., went to your parents to take a shower, back to your grandparents again, and then it decided that you were going to wash your truck the very first thing that morning at the fire station where you happened to be at the time the call came in.

Sheryl Houser was the one who could take your children from you. Your children were removed from your custody less than two weeks prior to the murder. Sheryl Houser was the one who could take the marital residence from you. You were removed from your own home less than two weeks prior to the murder. Finally, Sheryl Houser was the one person who could take your freedom from you. She was the complaining witness in a very serious felony charge that was filed two weeks prior to the murder.

Some of this evidence is stronger than other evidence. Some of this evidence may not be very convincing. And frankly, your defense counsel did an effective job at minimizing the effect of some of these points. But circumstantial or not, there was plenty of evidence for a jury to decide and find that you are guilty beyond a reasonable doubt.

I want to tell you and I want to tell the family of the victim that there's no sentence I can give here today that can put a value on Sheryl's life. The purpose of, of assigning a number of years in the Department of Corrections don't equate to the value of Sheryl's life.

I can't consider, well, is Sheryl worth 60 years or 55 years? I can't do that because no amount of years is worth a human life...

The Court also considers the fact that, as Ms. Fehr stated, the Fehr family and your children were left to pick up the pieces afterwards and your life continued for 27 years. You enjoyed freedom for 27 years. The Court takes that into consideration when fashioning a sentence as well.

Given all of the foregoing, the Court finds that an appropriate sentence in this case is a sentence of incarceration in the Illinois Department of Corrections of 55 years followed by an additional period of mandatory supervised release. That period would be for three years.

I wanted to hug Judge Koritz and cry just like I had done with Dana after the conviction but I couldn't. I've done it many times in my mind since then.

After all this time, it was really over.

AFTERWORD

I've said numerous times over the past 31 years that I was going to write a book.

This isn't uncommon, so many people have said they would do such a thing at various times in their lives. However, after the conviction, I really meant it. After years of researching and trying to learn everything there is to know about domestic violence, the abusers and their victims, I wanted to use that knowledge and my experience to help others. I always felt that Sheryl, who was a born sympathetic caregiver, would want to continue to help others if possible. Her death shouldn't be the end of her helping people.

Her story deserved to be told for what it was. People need to connect with others when they need hope. I believe that hope can be inspired in others by connections made through the sharing of personal stories. They need to know that they aren't the only one experiencing what they are going through during a difficult time. If I told my own personal story, perhaps others could gain the courage and have the hope to find the true inner peace that I've finally found.

I love to talk to others about my experiences and what I have learned from them. So I launched a business. After I graduated law school, one of the reasons I kept my maiden name was because I had some aspirations of becoming a judge and I couldn't think of a better name for one than Judge Fehr. As life unfolded, the judge aspirations waned. However, desires to own my own business still existed.

I launched Fehr Advocacy and Consultation with a mission to provide advice and education to others based on what I have learned from my research and years of experience navigating my family's journey to get justice for Sheryl. As a trained litigator who loves to tell stories, I share mine to provide hope to others. Writing a book that tells this story from beginning to end has formed the foundation for Fehr Advocacy and Consultation to execute its mission and vision.

I thought when I launched Fehr Advocacy and Consultation that my learnings had all happened along the way. Never underestimate the power of hindsight. In writing this book, I reviewed the two tubs of my old notes, and letters, and 5 boxes of files from Bob's representation of Sheryl and my family. These went from her divorce to the settlement of the wrongful death case and then my notes, e-mails, and court documents of the most recent investigation, through the arrest, conviction, sentencing, and post-trial motions. Looking at the case thirty years after her death brought an entirely different perspective. The emotions of her death were no longer raw, hope prevailed, and Greg was in prison.

In writing this book, I talked to Roger. I thought meeting with him would not only help me write a more complete book, it would also help me put to rest some of the feelings I had about why it took so long to bring this case to trial.

Part of me is angry it took so long for Greg to face justice, but another part of me says, "Thank God he didn't, it all worked out." My mother always says that Roger is a nice man, but maybe he wouldn't have won. We had to wait 27 years, but in the end it was worth it.

I have absolutely no ill feelings towards Roger. Rather I have great respect for all the things he did back then. In my heart, I believe the timing was just not right. If it had been tried in the past and we had lost, where would we be today? I doubt the boys would all be college educated, with jobs and families and a wealth of love surrounding them. I sincerely doubt that I would have learned all I have learned and would not be helping others as I am today and perhaps most importantly, I doubt I would have found the solace that I have so recently discovered with so much more of my life to live.

I shed a lot of tears, and felt emotions ranging from happy, angry, and sad countless times and spent a lot of time with my counselor trying to make sense of it all. The result—a true inner peace I never knew could exist. My life has been, and still is, far from perfect, which I always wanted it to be. But after having shared my story with all its imperfections and hearing others' stories with all their imperfections, I no longer attach shame to those imperfections because shame cannot attach to the things we admit to ourselves.

Writing this book certainly doesn't mean to my family what it means to me. Some members of my family wish I had just let things be. They probably believe it is easier to forget and ignore than remember and explore. I get it, everyone reacts differently and I don't want to offend those with that opinion. We are each entitled to our own. Julie did two victim impact panels with me and Lisa and told me afterwards she could never do it again, that she is proud of me and wants to support me, but it makes her too sad and upset to think about it. Lisa is probably somewhere in between where I'm at and Julie is. However, Julie, Lisa, and I have lived up to the pact we made in the back of the limo at the cemetery the day we buried Sheryl. We'll always take care of her boys and no matter what, even if we all don't like each other all the time, we won't fight with each other. We truly have lived this for 31 years and I know nothing can stop us from going to our graves living up to this. For this, I'm proud.

I wondered many times throughout this process if I was a bad person for doing this; for telling my story when others wanted to forget theirs. While my mother has not expressed this to me in words, I know deep down she is proud of me and my desire to allow Sheryl's story to be told to help others. One of my hopes is that my family knows this was my way of healing and that they can respect the process I needed to go through. I hope they know that no matter what, I love them and always will.

My hope for all of you who read my story is that you too can find the same inner peace that I have found. And never give up. I never did, and Dana and Elizabeth didn't either.

PHOTOS

The house where we grew up outside Farmer City, Illinois

The Fehr girls with "Tiny Tim" their pet racoon.
Sheryl dressed him in doll clothes for the photo.

Renee, Sheryl and Lisa with their pet rabbit.

*Victor and Phyllis with Sheryl when she
graduated from nurses training.*

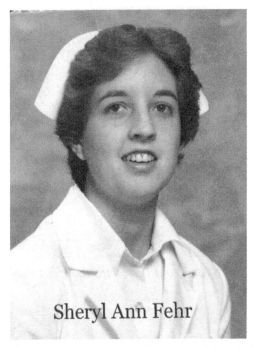

Sheryl Ann Fehr

Sheryl's graduation from Nurses Training Photo.

*Sheryl and Greg at our house. That sad
look stands out to me in hindsight.*

*Back row: Mike, Lisa, Dad, Sheryl with their second boy
and Greg. Front row: Julie, Mom with Sheryl's oldest, her
first grandchild, and me behind mom and in front of dad.*

*Christmas at our house. Greg and
Sheryl with their oldest son.*

Sheryl at Julie's wedding.

*Renee and her kids with Sheryl's oldest
at his 8th grade graduation.*

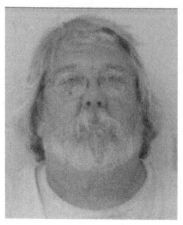

Greg's mug shot after the arrest for Sheryl's murder.

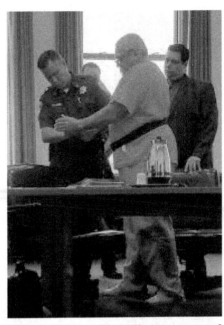

Greg and Piatt County Sheriff at a pre-trial hearing.

*State's Attorney Dana Rhoades and Assistant
State's Attorney Elizabeth Dobson.*

State's Attorney Dana Rhoades and Renee at a pretrial hearing.

Greg cleaned up for his murder trial.

Greg being led to the prison van after his conviction.

Dad, Mom, Julie, Lisa and Renee outside the Piatt County Courthouse after Greg's sentencing hearing.

Mom proudly displaying her "Book of Sheryl" to the judge after bravely reading her impact statement.

Lawrence Correctional Institute where Greg first served time after his conviction. Renee and her kids where flying to hear Kelly Sundberg, a domestic violence survivor and author of "Goodbye Sweet Girl" speak when I looked down and there was the prison where Greg was incarcerated.

The Fehr Family Christmas 2020. Top Row is Jim, Lisa, Dad, Mom, Jeff, Julie and Renee and Joe. Bottom is nearly all our kids and Sheryl's along with their kids. Sheryl always wanted a baby girl. Each of her boys' first child was a baby girl.

Renee and her kids – Mickael and Alexander with their dogs Johnny (yes, named after their father and Russell) after obtaining justice for Sheryl.

For More News About Renee Fehr and Brian Whitney, Signup For Our Newsletter:

http://wbp.bz/newsletter

Word-of-mouth is critical to an author's long-term success. If you appreciated this book please leave a review on the Amazon sales page:

http://wbp.bz/wheelsjusticea

**AVAILABLE FROM GIL VALLE, BRIAN
WHITNEY, AND WILDBLUE PRESS!**

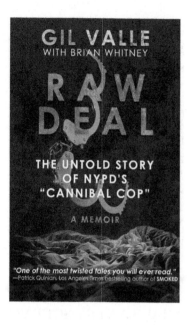

RAW DEAL by GIL VALLE and BRIAN WHITNEY

Raw Deal is the untold story of former New York City
police officer Gil Valle, who in 2012 became known
throughout the world as "The Cannibal Cop." It is part
the controversial saga of a man who was imprisoned
for "thought crimes," and a look into a world of
dark sexuality and violence that most readers don't
know exists, except maybe in their nightmares.

http://wbp.bz/rawdeala

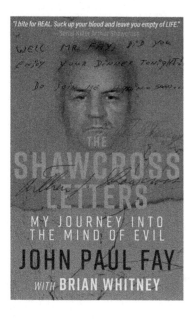

Made in the USA
Las Vegas, NV
19 September 2021